My Rescued Golden

My Rescued Golden

◆

True Stories of
Rescued Golden Retrievers
and the People Who Love Them

Marjorie McHann

Writers Club Press
San Jose New York Lincoln Shanghai

My Rescued Golden
True Stories of
Rescued Golden Retrievers
and the People Who Love Them

Writers Club Press
an imprint of iUniverse, Inc.

For information address:
iUniverse, Inc.
5220 S. 16th St., Suite 200
Lincoln, NE 68512
www.iuniverse.com

ISBN: 0-595-24989-2

Printed in the United States of America

For all the Volunteers
Of all the
Golden Retriever Rescue Groups

Contents

FOREWORD

I was surprised to be asked to write an introduction for a book such as this one, as I've been more the admirer and supporter, than that of leader, in the Golden Rescue movement. As a practicing school psychologist, my presence in the school system has similarly been one of both champion and protector, advocating for a child's inherent strengths rather than his or her apparent deficiencies. My own convictions remain consistent, whether tending to children or animals, as I see little difference between that of throwaway dogs and throwaway children. Despite society's diminished expectations, these challenged youngsters and animals are, time and again, the ones making the most unique contributions.

Called upon to evaluate youngsters in distress, my goal has always remained the same—to convey their stories effectively, detailing just what a particular child's world looks like from his or her eyes. Likewise, authors such as Susan Chernak McElroy implore us to honor our own stories and truths about animals, listening to the tales animals have to tell us. For it is within this sphere of listening and sharing and affection for animals that she believes we can restore our spirits.

Celebrated veterinarian Allen M. Schoen has a vision for a society in which we cease to be owner and pet, human and animal, but are simply respected companions connected by a special unique bond, that of kindred spirits. The introduction that he provides in his seminal text, *Kindred Spirits: How the Remarkable Bond Between Humans & Animals Can Change the Way We Live*, details the wonders of a gifted Golden Retriever named Megan. Dr. Schoen, in fact, dedicated the book to Megan, having promised her as she lay dying that the wisdom he had gained from her would be shared with as many people as possible.

While Megan came to be one of Allen Schoen's most compelling teachers, it was truly a miracle that she found her way to him. Abandoned and gravely ill, she hung on during a painful recovery process as the good doctor took her in and helped her mend. In a special pact, he also promised that, should she survive, he would adopt her.

Well, Megan became an irreplaceable companion, actually accompanying Allen on his rounds. She watched and studied and then copied his behavior while he cared for other animals. And rather amazingly, Megan's empathic ability to connect with patients proved invaluable. Inspired by her contributions, Dr. Schoen becomes quite impassioned when asked for the best way to personally help a kindred spirit. This is his answer:

"Find an abandoned or a homeless or an abused animal friend and bring him or her into your life. Share your home with your new companion and provide as much love and nurturance as you can. Receive the same love and affection back and allow the two of you to grow together. Your life and the life of your friend—will never be the same. Your joy will be great and your souls will flourish. Their cup and yours will truly runneth over with love!"

◆   ◆   ◆

This is the heart behind the Dog Rescue movement, as hundreds of non-profit groups (for both mixed and pure breeds) provide medical care, rehabilitation, and forever homes for those animals that are neglected, abandoned, homeless, abused, or simply displaced due to unforeseen family circumstances.

The process can be a lengthy and costly one, as dogs are first provided with temporary shelter in foster homes while they are evaluated and treated medically. They are also given some training and assessed with respect to their temperament toward humans, children, other dogs, cats, etc. Finally, depending on a particular dog's difficulties or issues, the right adoptive home is found.

Rescue groups also work in the community to promote responsible pet guardianship and encourage the humane care and treatment of companion animals. A strong spay/neuter advocacy is seen in their education efforts through pet functions such as dog walks, dog shows, and pet expos.

Yet, the true beauty within our Golden Rescue community lies in the astonishing dedication of its volunteers working tirelessly as they endeavor to make a difference. These individuals display the patience of saints as they gently attempt to lessen the effects of previous physical or emotional traumas. They do not rigidly define a dog's worth or desirability by its outside beauty or swiftness in movement. Rather, they remain fixed on that inner essence and wonder of the canine spirit. And they perform miracles day in and day out, gaining strength from the power of the Human-Canine Bond.

In all honesty, the true champions—those defenders of rescue—are my heroes, as I find myself moved by their compassion and emotional resilience. Folks like Barb Justice, Intake & Fort Worth Area Foster Coordinator for the Golden Retriever Rescue of North Texas, who must come to grips with society's inhumanity, and yet at the same time remain focused on their ultimate rescue mission, mystify me. Of course, Barb is always quick to remind me of the joy that can only come from a *Rescued Golden*, sharing the following observations:

"The one idea I would like to promote about rescued dogs is that they are not recycled hand me downs. I have had the privilege to meet and even care for dogs that were so intelligent, athletic, devoted and loving that any breeder would give their eyeteeth to have them in their program. They bond with their humans as strongly, if not more so, than any puppy. And some truly seem to know that they are getting a second chance and are very, very grateful for that. The thing I love about rescue is watching a sad, broken little stalk blossom onto a gorgeous, healthy magnificent sunflower of an animal, walking proudly with tail held high. That is what it is all about. The 'before and after' photos can be dramatic!"

◆   ◆   ◆

Currently, my own furry homestead is rounded out by a feisty six-pound Rescue kitty, who only begrudgingly accepts the fact that she must share her life space with two rowdy Golden Retrievers. Interestingly, it was my Golden Ollie who, eight years ago, alerted me to her presence outside our window as she pitifully scavenged for food during a harsh period of ice storms.

Although my family has yet to be adorned by a Rescue Golden, I have had the special fortune to provide an emergency foster home. And, thankfully, the sad and hurting Golden Penny who turned up on my doorstep came to be a *lucky* Penny after all. Let me share her story…

A short time before Christmas 1998, I received a heartbreaking call from my pharmacist husband, telling me about a tragic situation. One of his good customers, who knew of his love for Goldens, hoped that he could help out with an elderly neighbor's Golden. This neighbor had been battling cancer for some time, and, as a result, was unable to give her gal Penny much love or attention. Sadly, the woman died, and now Penny was alone with no one to care for her. If a home could not be found, Penny would be euthanized.

We could not let that happen and immediately took Penny into our home. She was very needy due to several illnesses and a protracted time of neglect. She had no desire to play or to remain near my side, surely grieving all that had recently transpired in her life. Penny was a quiet and sorrowful gal, both her beauty and pain revealed through gorgeous deep brown eyes. I immediately contacted Mary Ellen Lunde, the exceptional Intake and Foster Home Coordinator from GRREAT, my own local Golden Rescue organization. She responded quickly and, within days, was at my door ready to transport Penny to her new foster home. We were so happy someone would be able to help bring her back to some health and happiness. Tears, which stung my eyes as I watched Mary Ellen drive off with Penny in tow, now return as the memory is revisited with this writing.

Debbie Iwanczuk provided this special gal with a loving and caring foster home for the next three months. In the *GRREAT News* Spring 1999 issue, she shared her fostering experience in a heartfelt article, entitled "Foster Tails." Many were touched by Debbie's article, including a dedicated and caring family from West Chester, Pennsylvania who knew that they could provide Penny with the life she so deserved.

Debbie detailed to the family Penny's intensive medical issues (thyroid problem, ear infections, arthritis, bladder infection, recurrent hot spots and itching that required a permanently affixed Elizabethan collar), knowing that a huge commitment would be necessary. However, rather than prove discouraging, it only increased their desire to finalize the adoption. You see, GRREAT had provided them a Golden dream in 1997 when they adopted a guy named Scholar, and now they had a perfect opportunity to show their gratitude by adopting a dog that no one else would take. This extraordinary family included stay-at-home mom Kate, dad Seth, two young boys, two cats, and, of course, Scholar. When Penny arrived at Seth and Kate's home, she did lots of exploring. Seeming to draw strength and energy from the children, her tail would wag furiously whenever they would talk to her.

The update I received a couple of years ago on Penny's progress was beyond my wildest hopes. No longer requiring a huge assortment of medicines, she was easily being maintained on a single medication for a thyroid deficiency. But, more importantly, the vet who had given Penny a mere six months to live advised the family that this now 10-year-old could be around for another four years or so. Amazing what a little love can do.

Remarkably, the family has since taken another hopeless case under their wings. Thirteen-year-old Sunny Girl, who allegedly only had weeks to live, was welcomed just as Penny had been. Now, twelve months later, this senior gem continues to shine, contentedly sharing her canine life space with Goldens Scholar and Penny.

◆   ◆   ◆

I always smile when reflecting on Allen Schoen's observation that *"G-d made dogs and then when he perfected them…he created Goldens."* Yet it is comforting that so many do share this faith in the *Golden Good*.

I agree with Milan Kundera when he insists, *"dogs are our link to paradise"* and believe that those who have discovered the powers of *The Bond* have increased the quality of their lives immeasurably. Certainly, the Human-*Golden* Bond is a powerful force, Goldens playing a pivotal role in improving one's health, independence, and quality of life. In fact, the breed continues to dominate the service field industry, many abandoned Goldens going on to become trusted assistance, detection and search & rescue dogs. Yet, for me, it is their timeless spirit and capacity to mimic our human qualities that makes the breed so endearing—our definition of *family* surely incomplete without a Golden's inclusion.

You are sure to be touched by the forty-six stories that follow in *My Rescued Golden*, these second-chance canines miraculously helping their new adoptive families grow even closer. For the lessons these furry angels teach us are never-ending, inspiring a new respect, appreciation and celebration of life.

Rochelle Lesser, CAS NCSP
Therapist and Consultant
Millersville Psychological Services
Millersville, Maryland

Creator, LIVE, LOVE & LAUGH with Golden Retrievers
A website celebrating the Human-Golden Bond
At Landofpuregold.com

ACKNOWLEDGMENTS

First of all, I am tremendously grateful to the Golden owners included in *My Rescued Golden* whose efforts made the book possible.

I'm indebted to my sister Rebecca Sydnor for her great ideas, creativity, and enthusiasm. And for his love and support, I thank my husband Mike.

Mary Hannington gave me valuable guidance throughout the project, for which I'm most grateful. In addition, she lent her extraordinary photographic skills for several of the pictures and produced the stories of her Golden friends Zack and Floyd.

Other people as well have given me encouragement and significant help in different ways. I would like to thank Sally Spaulding (RAGOM) for collecting and producing all the stories from her rescue organization. A sincere thank you to Mary Jungbluth (GRROW) for writing and managing the stories from her rescue group. Grateful thanks to Terese Barta (GRROW) for producing Coco's story. And I'm indebted to Rochelle Lesser for writing such an inspiring Foreword under a very tight deadline.

Finally, I salute the ones who give unconditional love and buoy me with their spirits and zest for life—my Goldens, Leo and Goldie; unknowingly they have given the most.

PHOTOGRAPHIC CREDITS

Hannah & Hunter Grimm *by* Mary Hannington

Annie Knoche *by* The Garden Studio Inc.

Ian Doyle *by* Aimee Miller

Merry Heart Norgood *by* Mary Jungbluth

Floyd Bass *by* Mary Hannington

Promise Hecker *by* Brenda Holzea

Kodiak Bourassa *by* Brenda Holzea

Memphis Hannington *by* Mary Hannington

Goldie McHann *by* Marjorie McHann

Dillon Mahoney *by* Marjorie McHann

Nutmeg Randall *by* TheKnoxville News-Sentinel Company

Zack Sankar *by* Mary Hannington

Cover Photo of Daisy McHann *by* Marjorie McHann

INTRODUCTION

I've always found great satisfaction in the process of fixing up things and restoring them to their greatest potential. As a nurse, I help people recover to their optimum level of health; as a developer, I transform tired houses into sought-after dwellings; and as a rescuer, I turn throwaway dogs into somebody's best loved companion. It's very rewarding to leave something better off than when I found it.

As volunteers for Tennessee Valley Golden Retriever Rescue, my husband Mike and I have acted as a foster family for dozens of golden retrievers that needed a safe, nurturing environment while they awaited their forever home. Some of these golden retrievers were healthy, happy dogs that were adopted within days. But others were sick in body and spirit and stayed with us for months while they healed and developed the self-confidence they needed to adjust to an adopting family.

Words cannot adequately describe the satisfaction that comes from rescuing these golden retrievers in often horrendous condition from sometimes nightmarish situations, watching them recover and thrive, and orchestrating their adoption into carefully selected families that revere them as the treasures they are. The satisfaction comes not only from saving the golden retrievers, but also from witnessing the joy they bring to their new families.

The high rate of successful adoptions among golden retriever rescue groups stems from the fact that the needs of the golden retrievers are considered first and foremost; after all they've been through, it's essential that the rescued Goldens will be guaranteed a safe and happy future. Adoption applicants are closely screened to eliminate those with a history of irresponsible pet ownership, those who won't let their

Golden live inside, and those who don't pass muster during a home visit.

In addition, applicants are matched with the Golden of their choice only if they can meet the specific needs of that dog. Can they provide the perfect home for the Golden who needs other dogs to be happy? For the Golden who prefers to be an "only dog?" For the Golden who wouldn't be happy without children in his life? For the high energy Golden who craves long sessions of fetching the ball? And so on. In my experience, adopting families are grateful for this careful process, because it benefits them as well as the Golden. How many times have they laughingly remarked, *"This is just like adopting a child!"*

My 40+ foster Goldens have all been adopted by very special families who experienced firsthand the joy of sharing their lives with a rescued Golden. These "happy beginnings" are repeated thousands of times every year with rescued golden retrievers across the country, and thus was born the idea for this book.

A loving celebration of the emotional bond between rescued Goldens and their humans, this heartwarming collection of photographs and stories conveys every aspect of the humor, devotion, fun and inevitable sorrow that exist within this special relationship. And honored are the volunteers of the rescue organizations that dedicate their time, energy, money, and hearts to this noble endeavor.

Here, in the words of adopters writing about their rescued Goldens, you'll meet Dakota who was saved from the streets and now brings joy as a therapy dog; Promise who got a second chance at life after surviving years in a breeding kennel; Sproul who became a bomb detection Police K-9 dog after being surrendered by her owners for being "too energetic;" Ozzie who was rescued from the kill shelter to transform his first-time dog owner into a "real dog person;" Nutmeg who saves lives as a search and rescue dog after being labeled as "overly aggressive" by her former owner; Hope who was saved from death in a backyard breeding nightmare to inspire her adopting family to leave Manhattan following another nightmare September 11, 2001;—and dozens more.

These eloquent pictures and wonderful stories will touch anyone whose heart has ever belonged to a Golden.

Editor's note: All profits from this book will be donated to the Golden retriever rescue organizations that rescued the Goldens in these stories.

Carol Guenther and Coco

COCO

Golden Retriever Rescue of Wisconsin

Coco almost never got a chance at life. Because she was born with a deformed front paw, her breeder nearly had her destroyed at birth. But the young pup managed to escape an early death only to find a sad life being passed from one home to the next. Finally, at the age of 18 months, she was surrendered to the golden retriever rescue group and adopted by our family.

Coco's paw doesn't keep her from doing anything she wants. She's very exuberant and loves to run and play and chase balls. She loves everyone and anyone who will give her attention. She also loves to snuggle up with people and uses her paw like a hand to pull someone in to cuddle. Although an accident of nature deprived her of a normal paw, it more than compensated her with a beautiful face and sweet, loving disposition.

Coco is changing people's views about disabilities, her first success being my own family. Initially, their reaction was "we don't want a crippled dog," but I persisted because I knew Coco was the dog for us. What I find interesting now is that nobody in the family even mentions the paw anymore. I believe their reactions are typical of how people generally regard those with disabilities. At first, we're put off by someone who's different. But we stop seeing the disability once we begin to see the whole person. Although my family no longer notices the paw, it continues to draw attention from other people who ask, "What happened to your dog's paw?" This gives me the opportunity to subtly educate them about disabilities in general. To Coco, her paw is not a disability. Since she was born with it, it's completely "normal."

As a registered nurse, I work for a hand surgeon who specializes in helping children with hands affected by birth defects or accidents. After she's completed her Good Citizenship and Therapy Dog Certification, Coco will become a therapy dog at the children's clinic. This little dog with the misshapen paw will have the chance to help kids deal with their own hand problems. The puppy that started life as a breeder's throwaway looks forward to a future career as a therapy dog and a purpose in life.

—Carol Guenther

Stephanie Glazer and Dakota

DAKOTA

Golden Re-Triever Rescue of New Jersey

When I first saw Dakota, I thought he was the strangest-looking golden retriever I'd ever seen. He looked like one of those children's puzzles, where the body parts of different animals are mixed to create new, impossible creatures. His front half didn't match his small rear half, which was skinny and lacked any muscle tone. All the angles in his rear half were off, so his bad leg turned out at the hip, turned out further at the knee, his tail came out of his side, and he could barely put any weight on his crooked crippled leg which he dragged along like a second tail.

While wandering the streets, Dakota had been hit by a car, suffering extensive injuries to his rear leg and pelvis. The Humane Society saved him and donated the surgeries to repair his injuries, but when the treatment was finished he looked really weird. When his owner didn't claim Dakota, the rescue group accepted him and I agreed to foster him until he was adopted, so off I went with my Golden females Daisy and Sammie to collect this sorry excuse for a dog.

After a couple of days, Dakota was responding to his new name and obeying all the usual commands. Then, on the third night, while I was walking all three dogs, my Daisy suddenly spotted a squirrel and bolted, knocking me to the ground and shredding my knee on the gravel road. Daisy's only interest was the squirrel, and easy-going Sammie was oblivious to everything except the good smells along the path. It was the new kid, Dakota, who immediately stuck his face in mine, kissing me, nudging me, trying to help me get up and (I swear) saying with sincere concern "ARE YOU OKAY?" It was at that moment I realized the bond between this funny little crooked boy and me was so strong that no adopting family would ever meet my approval because no one would ever be good enough for him.

Dakota has been here ever since, adopted by us and, yes, he's a mama's boy and I wouldn't have it any other way. He's filled out and rebuilt lost muscle and gallops like the wind through the yard with his sisters. As a certified therapy dog, Dakota brings his special magic to the residents of a care facility for mentally challenged adults. He's in great health with a "career" and a very bright future, and we feel so lucky that he came into our lives. Dakota is living proof that when life gives you lemons you make lemonade! He's the four-legged love of my life and is totally devoted to me in return.

—*Stephanie Glazer*

Debbie Grimm and Hannah & Hunter

HANNAH & HUNTER

Golden Retriever Rescue of Michigan

Hannah was used for breeding and hunting. Hunter is one of Hannah's "babies." The two of them were the "house dogs" for several years, but then a couple of Hannah's other pups took over their places in the house and that's when Hannah and Hunter were relegated to the outside. They were tied to a barn way out in the back and forgotten. They were fed, but that's about all. Hannah and Hunter lived this way for several years until they were released to the rescue group at the ages of 8 and 6.

Hunter was quickly adopted and, soon after, Mike and I adopted Hannah. When we first met her, we were shocked at Hannah's appearance because she was just skin and bones and her coat was dull and very thin. But she came trotting right over to us with her tail wagging and those big brown eyes smiling up at us and we knew she was the one for us! In no time, Hannah bounced back, gained weight, and grew out a lustrous golden coat. She became our constant companion wherever we went and it was hard to imagine how we ever got along without her. But we always wondered what happened to Hunter and whether or not Hunter missed her "mom" and Hannah her "daughter."

A year later, we learned her new family had returned Hunter to the rescue group. Without any hesitation, Mike and I knew that Hunter was meant to be with us and we adopted her right away and brought her home. Hannah and Hunter had a joyous "family reunion" and the rest is history!

These two "girls" of ours are now 10 and 12 years old and I cannot say enough for the joy they have brought to our lives. I know some people think a dog this age would be no fun, but that couldn't be further from the truth. When given the chance, they can still run like lightning. Hannah has a pile of stuffed animals she digs into and plays with and Hunter still "pounces" on her bone when she's excited and wants to play. They just love going for walks and rides in the car and they love to snuggle with us on the den floor in the evenings. They love each other, and we love them. Adopting a puppy is great fun for the right family, but we think adopting a Senior is the only way to go.

We know the day will come when we have to say "good-bye" to our girls, but the love, the paws wrapped around our arms, and the cold-nosed kisses will never be forgotten.

—*Debbie Grimm*

Jan Knoche and Annie

ANNIE

Golden Recovery Retrieving Retrievers Rescue—Midwest

Annie was our first foster dog. When she came to us she was suffering from malnutrition and was scared of everything. She was 7 years old and had lived her life having puppies in a puppymill and had all the emotional scars that come with the territory.

We soon fell in love with Annie and let her blossom at her own pace, which was very slow. At first, she was so shy, the only way we could take her picture was with a zoom lens. Even then we had to be fast before she ran away so, as you can see, this portrait is a tribute to how far Annie has come. She's still very shy with people she doesn't know, but each day she becomes a little more trusting.

Everyone says that Annie is a true Rags to Riches Story. We call her the Duchess because she loves to lay in her bed with her favorite stuffed toys and watch the world go by. She's the first one out the door when it's time to go for a walk, and she adores running and playing with her two Golden brothers.

Annie is very special because of the way she helps us with our steady stream of foster dogs, which are usually puppies. She teaches them how to have respect for her and, as a result, they learn doggie manners and get the socialization they lacked before coming to rescue. When she feels the time is right, she'll play with them, but when she needs to, she'll make sure they behave. By the time the puppies get to their forever home, they have a good foundation on which to grow, thanks to Annie. We're always amazed at this special knack she has, which we suspect has come from having many litters of puppies. Annie is giving back to rescue over and over. Three years after leaving her old existence behind, Annie is living proof there can be a happy life after a terrible one.

—Jan Knoche

Robin Williams and Ben

GENTLE BEN

Triad Golden Retriever Rescue

Last September I began thinking about what it would be like to have a Golden Retriever in our family. We already had 4 cocker spaniels, 2 cats, and a 3-year-old toddler, so it was like asking, "Do you need another hole in your head?" Obviously, the answer was yes, because I couldn't put the thought out of my mind. A puppy was out of the question, so I sought out a rescue group and that's where I found Gentle Ben. A stray, he had been saved from the streets by the rescue group and treated for a severe case of heartworms.

I loved Ben the moment I saw him and so did my husband and toddler, Dalton. Ben is a big Golden, weighing 104 pounds with not an ounce of fat! The first time I took Ben to meet my vet, he exclaimed, "Now that's a dog!" Although it took a few weeks, our cockers and the cats finally adjusted to Ben. But the first month he was "home," Ben swallowed the arms off his canvas chew man, the cover of his tennis ball, and a slice of cake wrapped in aluminum foil! I'll never forget the first time I heard Ben bark. It was at the mailman's car and I just about left my body completely! What a voice! I was accustomed to the cocker spaniel bark, wow! Nobody in their right mind will ever break into our house!

Ben is so good with our toddler, Dalton. I have actually seen Dalton bite Ben's tail and Ben just looked at me as if to say, "It's OK mom, I can handle him." They lie on the floor together watching TV with Dalton's head on Ben's big chest like a pillow. At bedtime when we're saying our prayers, Ben is right there beside us and, if I get too long winded, he starts barking at me. I have rheumatoid arthritis and, because Ben is so large, he was a little hard for me to manage on the leash. Ben's foster mom recommended the Gentle Leader and it worked like a charm; within 10 minutes, Ben was matching my pace stride for stride.

This spring, Ben and I were certified by The Delta Society International as an Animal Assisted Therapy Team and now we visit the rehabilitation facility, where Ben bring smiles to many faces and comforts those who need a touch from a real *"heart of gold."* I am so proud of this big golden dog with the huge paws and even bigger heart. He is my canine soul mate and I love him dearly.

—*Robin Williams*

Sandi Brown and Frosty & Maggie

FROSTY

Norcal Golden Retriever Rescue

We'll never know Frosty's start in life or her real name. Was she a happy puppy, well loved and fed or were her first 12 years full of misery? Fortunately for me, I'll never know. A few days before Christmas, Frosty was found on a deserted road, shot in the head and left for dead, probably a botched euthanasia job. A passerby following a trail of blood found the old dog and rushed her to a nearby vet clinic where, despite her condition, she attempted to sit up and wag her old broken tail. The bullet missed her brain but passed through her ear into her jaw, paralyzing the left side of her face. Following emergency surgery, she was transferred to the Humane Society for followup care and subsequently released to the Norcal Golden Retriever Rescue Group.

On Christmas Eve, I sat down to read the newspaper online, as I did every evening. The headlines shouted: ***Dog Survives Shooting, But Faces Euthanasia***. Shocked, I read every word of the story and shuddered at the cruelty done to this old Golden and the irony that she would be euthanized unless someone adopted her. Surely someone would come forward and give her a good home. Myself, I already had two golden retrievers, Maggie who I purchased as a puppy and Sam who I adopted from the rescue group. Besides, I just didn't have time for a third Golden, what with my job as a nurse and my volunteer work at the Humane Society and Santa Rosa dog parks. The last thing I needed was to have to buy more dog food, pay more vet bills, and make more room for another Golden. Surely someone else would take care of her. But I couldn't get her out of my mind and so the day after Christmas I went to the shelter just to see her.

Despite the graphic description in the newspaper article, I was totally unprepared for what I would find. The old Golden smelled rank from chronic skin infections, and sparse tufts of hair barely warmed her body, a result of years of neglect. The left side of her face drooped from partial paralysis, a baseball-sized tumor hung from her back leg, and her tail was crooked from an old injury. Green drainage spilled from both eyes, evidence of longstanding infections, and the vet reported a heart murmur, a lung tumor, and cataracts, among other ailments. She was pitiful. But as I approached, she greeted me sweetly and allowed me to pet her and touch her all over, the old tail wagging and the grayed nose nuzzling me. My heart broke, thinking of what had happened to this trusting old Golden, and I decided that she would be coming home with me.

The following day I brought her home and named her Frosty for her beautiful white face and the light holiday snow that fell that day in her honor. Frosty loved my other Goldens and they loved her. Eventually, her coat grew in red and shiny and her mouth improved to the point she could carry around her tennis ball. Her happiest times were riding in my car with her head out the window sniffing the smells and feeling the wind on her face. One of her favorite places was the dog park, where she would lie in the sun and greet the people who came by just to meet "the famous dog." We became inseparable and she went with me everywhere. Finally, though, the untreatable lung tumor took its toll on her old body and I helped her pass in peace as she lay in my arms. Frosty's final ten months had been as happy as could be. In spite of all her disabilities and infirmities, she had a heart and spirit bigger than life. She wasn't going to let anything get her down. Every day Frosty showed us how to live in the moment, appreciate the little things, and be happy. I loved her dearly.

Despite a large reward offered by the community, the perpetrator of Frosty's cruel injury was never found. But shortly after I adopted her, I spoke to him in a letter that was printed in the newspaper: *"An old animal, like an old person, has enough trouble living with arthritis, cataracts, skin problems, and, in this dog's case, heart and lung disease. You had to paralyze her face so she can't feel on that side, close her eye properly, hear out of that ear, or hold her tennis ball tightly. But the old girl goes on, trotting, swinging that broken old tail and smiling that smile only a Golden can give. She found a good home with some nice people. Her final days will be full and safe and peaceful. And you know what? If she saw you today, she would go up and lick your hand: Goldens are like that."*

—*Sandi Brown*

Priscilla Parish and Lilly

LILLY

Gold Ribbon Golden Retriever Rescue

Lilly came from a divorced family. Her dad didn't have time for her, and her mom just didn't want her. She left Lilly outside all day long without any love. She was 10 months old when I brought her home.

Lilly is my baby girl. Three years later and we are still inseparable. She goes with me everywhere! I think she's the only dog in the world that doesn't look out the window while riding in the car. Instead, she faces me. Every time we stop at a stoplight, she paws my arm and pulls it to her belly for me to scratch.

Her hips are starting to hurt her, so it's a little tougher for her to get in and out of the car with me. I don't care what it takes for me to give her a happy, fulfilled life. She is unconditional with me, and I will always be that way for her. Lilly has truly blessed my life.

—Priscilla Parish

OUACHITA TECHNICAL COLLEGE

Sandy Knox and Fancy

FANCY

Golden Retriever Rescue of Michigan

Fancy is a very special golden retriever. A bright, vivacious, curious, courageous, and affectionate five-year-old, she was only two when I adopted her from the rescue group. Back then she was rather skinny and would spin in circles at about 100 mph whenever she got excited, which was often. She still spins occasionally, but only when she is really excited.

Fancy is, in many ways, a typical Golden. Her toy of choice is a tennis ball, which she'll retrieve for hours on end. In the summer, her priority turns to retrieving her float in the water, and there simply aren't enough hours in a day to exhaust the joy that comes from that activity. Fancy's good with other dogs but they mostly take a back seat to humans. She passed obedience school with flying colors and does pretty well in the obedience area given that her owner isn't nearly as consistent as she should be. She's also active in the Pet Visitation Program and visits the hospital, the cancer center, and a senior's residence once a month. Fancy makes me laugh every day.

I suppose by now you're thinking that Fancy is just another great Golden. But, you see, what makes Fancy so exceptional is the fact that she's totally blind. She's been blind from birth so being blind doesn't seem to bother her at all. Fancy is the shining example of the fact that you CAN make lemonade out of the lemons that life deals you. She reminds you every day that obstacles are meant to be overcome. When you bump into something you shake it off and carry on. If you get caught in a dilemma, like a bunch of trees in the bush, you keep going until you figure out how to get into the open. She reminds you that life is too short to miss a single solitary minute, so get out and experience everything you can.

Fancy lived happily with her "Daddy" until his bride-to-be issued the ultimatum and Fancy was surrendered to the golden retriever rescue group. I guess it's extraordinary that I have Fancy at all given the "illogicals" of our story. There's no logic to explain why I logged onto the Golden rescue website that day. There's no logic to explain why the rescue group waived their "no long distance adoption" policy. And there's no logic to explain why I decided to bring the scrawny, spinning creature home. Mostly, I think that God just wanted Fancy and me to get together. Whatever the logic I'm certainly glad we connected, as I can't imagine life without her.

—Sandy Knox

Alison Doyle and Ian

IAN

Peppertree Golden Retriever Rescue

One morning I received a call from our rescue group coordinator asking me if I would go by the animal shelter to pick up an elderly golden retriever and foster him until an adopting home could be found. The shelter considered him unadoptable due to a large tumor on his left thigh, and he was out of time and overdue to be euthanized.

I arrived at the shelter that morning and found a very special old Golden. Although Ian was obviously in pain from the grotesque tumor, he looked up at me pleadingly and gave me his paw, and I fell in love with him right on the spot. He was supposed to be my foster dog, but I knew he had found his forever home with me.

Ian underwent extensive surgery on September 11, 2001 to remove the 13-pound tumor from his thigh. For me and the other members of the rescue group, Ian was a ray of hope in the midst of that horrific day.

True to the maxim that first impressions are usually right, Ian is a special dog. He loves everyone he meets and his tail never stops wagging. I am so grateful for him. When people tell me how nice I was to rescue him, I tell them he has done more for me than I ever did for him. Ian has reminded me that you can't measure love in years. It seems like he's been with me forever. He is just a wonderful old boy.

—Alison Doyle

Nancy Norgood and Merry Heart

MERRY HEART

Golden Retriever Rescue of Wisconsin

Despite her name, Merry Heart did not always have a merry heart. Labeled as "breeding stock," she lived in a dark, unventilated barn with 60 other dogs for seven years before being saved by the rescue group. Untreated ear infections, broken teeth, fleas, intestinal parasites, and physical punishment had taken a toll. She didn't know how to play, a waving hand made her cower for protection and her eyes were filled with fear. Yet, despite the deplorable treatment she had endured, her spirit remained and her "merry heart" slowly began to respond to the tender nurturing of her foster family. For weeks, I had been waiting to adopt Merry Heart. Finally, the big day arrived and she came home with me to begin her new life.

Merry Heart has been with me for almost a year now. Her once dull, coarse coat is now shiny and soft, and her former scrubby tail is full and plume-like. The arthritis that made it difficult to hop inside a car or climb the steps is no longer apparent, because her medical needs are being met. She has a lively spirit, a mischievous nature, and a playful spring in her step. But the most amazing transformation is in her eyes. At first, they were small and expressionless, never wide open, but more like narrow slits as a result of years spent in the dark with no exposure to daylight. Gradually, Merry Heart's eyes adjusted to the light, and now they are big, brown, and beautiful! But one thing hasn't changed. True to her mothering instinct, she has chosen from her large toy collection a small stuffed bear for her substitute puppy. She gently carries "puppy" as if it were her very own and often nudges it close to her when she sleeps.

Several months after Merry Heart came to live with me, I had brain surgery for an aneurysm and had to live in an assisted living facility for a few weeks. A friend brought Merry Heart to visit often and she was such a blessing, warming the hearts of all the residents who lived there. Racing through the hallways with a stolen stuffed animal in her mouth, she made even the grouchy residents laugh! She had the heart of everyone who met her!

Now I'm back home again with Merry Heart. It's just the two of us, so we're always together. We take daily walks and afternoon naps and rides in the car. What's really fun is to sit in the backyard and watch her chase the squirrels and chipmunks. I am so lucky to have Merry Heart and to be alive.

—Nancy Norgood

Shannon Bass and Floyd

FLOYD

Golden Retriever Rescue of Michigan

My husband Daryl is not a dog person. When I told him I wanted to get one, he showed me a picture of a breed he would consider. It was a Golden. We're now on our second rescue Golden, Floyd.

When we first met Floyd, all we were told was that his age was somewhere between two and three years old. He seemed to know that Daryl was the one he had to impress. I just wanted a dog. Floyd went straight to Daryl, put his head on his lap and stayed there while Daryl petted him.

Floyd is a terrific dog, a real goofball with a distinct personality. No paper napkin is safe. He'll snatch them from your lap, your hand, or even the table. He also loves to lick people. One day I was taking a shower when all of a sudden I felt something warm on my leg, scaring me practically out of my skin. When I finally opened my eyes, there was Floyd. He had moved aside the curtain and stuck his head in the shower!

Floyd likes to be where we are and will follow us from room to room. If we're in different rooms, he lays on the floor between them, so that he can keep an eye on the both of us. We suspect that he may have a little Afghan in him, his nose is long and his coat is somewhat pale. He has the Golden temperament though; he's never met a person that he doesn't like, and is sure he's a lap dog.

—Shannon Bass

Emily and Alex Krenzke and Buster

BUSTER

Golden Retriever Rescue of Wisconsin

We didn't own a dog, especially since our 10-year-old son Alex was very afraid of them. We once had to leave a house we were visiting because he was afraid of their toy poodle! However, Alex had always seemed most tolerant of Golden Retrievers (I suspect because of their gentle nature) so when we finally decided to get a dog, we began our search with the Golden Retriever Rescue of Wisconsin. That's when we learned about Buster.

Buster was five years old when he was surrendered to a shelter because his family could no longer afford the vet bills. He had chronic, untreated ear infections that left his ears looking like cauliflora; his draining eyes were surrounded by bare, leathery skin that gave him the appearance of an old dog; and his skin was so itchy that his constant scratching had left him with open, infected sores. Buster was rescued from the shelter by GRROW and treated for hypothyroidism, which was the underlying cause of his ear, eye, and skin problems. After five years of suffering through this disease without a diagnosis, Buster was on his way to becoming healthy and free of infection.

We heard from his foster mom about Buster, and he sounded perfect for us. So we sent the "hard heart" among us, my husband Richard, to see if Buster was as perfect as he sounded. Well, on that very first visit, Buster found his way into Richard's newly softened heart, and we all went down for the "final test" the following weekend. Buster charmed all of us, including the usually timid Alex.

Buster has been with us now for a year. We feel totally blessed to have been entrusted with the care of such a wonderful Golden. He never gets into anything inappropriate and handles our two career family schedules without a hitch. His ears have cleared, his skin infections healed and his hypothyroidism is controlled with a pill. Our dog groomer specializes in Goldens and she tells us he's one of the nicest dogs she's ever seen!

Buster just loves the kids and snuggles whenever he can. His favorite thing to do is fetch tennis balls and will do so until he drops of exhaustion if you let him! Buster wants nothing more than to be well cared for and to be with us. His gentle, quiet, and unassuming manners have cured Alex of his fear of dogs. This is truly the "next beginning" for him and for us.

—*Karen Krenzke*

Suzanne Leroux and Porter

PORTER

Golden Retriever Rescue of Wisconsin

I adopted 6-month-old Porter from the Golden Retriever Rescue of Wisconsin and picked him up on a warm spring morning after a 4-month wait for the perfect dog. A stray, he had been saved from the animal shelter by the rescue group and, shortly after, diagnosed with hip dysplasia.

I knew in my heart when I went to meet Porter the first time that he was the perfect dog for me. I was looking for a medium-sized Golden that was good with children, because he would be responsible for entertaining my nieces and nephews when they came to visit.

Due to Porter's hip dysplasia, his activity was restricted and he wasn't allowed to jump, run or play fetch. That was a most challenging order to follow. After all, he was still a puppy and what puppy does not want to jump, run or play fetch? Finally this summer, Porter had both his Triple Pelvic Osteotomy (TPO) surgeries and has recovered from both surgeries without incident. Now he's back to his old self: running, jumping and fetching any and every ball he can get his mouth on.

Porter is a beautiful, sweet, mellow and gentle Golden, and I am very pleased to have him as part of my family. His love for any human makes him one very popular dog when we have visitors. He also "looks out" for my guests that stay for the night by sleeping at the foot of their bed. They welcome him with open arms and are pleased that he shows such a loyalty to them. He usually sleeps in his own bed at the foot of my bed and I do miss him on those nights.

Although the four-month wait seemed like forever, I would like to thank GRRoW for realizing that Porter was a perfect match for me. We were meant to be together forever. GRRoW also helped offset the costs of the surgeries through the Gracie Fund, and I am sincerely thankful for all their help. Porter can now run, jump, fetch and play like a puppy.

—*Suzanne Leroux*

Kim Hecker and Promise

PROMISE

Golden Retriever Rescue of Wisconsin

Promise was one of 5 golden retrievers that were saved by the rescue group from a notorious Missouri puppymill. Promise arrived at my home late on a warm spring night, almost catatonic with fear and acting like no dog I'd ever known. Mindful of my promise to foster her, I brushed aside my doubts and accepted the responsibility of caring for her until she was adopted.

Having spent the last four years in a small cage producing puppies, Promise was fearful of open spaces and tried to hide herself in the farthest dark corners of my home. She'd never been touched, hugged, or cuddled, and when I reached out to her with love, she'd startle, expecting to be hurt. But the saddest testament to her life of pain was the empty, emotionless, vacant expression in her eyes.

Two months passed and Promise slowly adjusted to the mechanics of life in my household, but she still hadn't shown any emotion or love toward me. Her life of solitary confinement had rendered her clueless about living with humans, and she preferred the company of my other two Goldens, Mandy and Murphy. Then one sunny afternoon, I sat cross-legged in the flowerbed pulling weeds while the three Goldens amused themselves behind me in another part of the yard. After a few minutes, I became aware of a presence and turned to see Promise standing nearby, watching me. Slowly I extended my hand and she crept close enough to touch my fingers with her nose. At that moment, we connected emotionally for the first time, and I decided then and there to adopt her and keep her safe forever.

Promise has been with me a year now. She takes her cues from my other Goldens and knows that I'm safe and won't hurt her. At obedience school, she learned basic commands and some confidence, and now she comes to me for petting and accepts treats from my hand. These days, Promise actually smiles; her tail is always wagging and her eyes are bright and happy.

But I wasn't always sure of a happy ending. Promise's spirit was so broken, I didn't know if I could ever love her enough to make up for all the hurts and harm she endured at the puppymill. But Promise taught me the real meaning of patience and perseverance. We still have a long way to go together, this is just our beginning, and I Promise she will have a healthy, happy, golden life.

—Kim Hecker

Nick Maurer and Charlie

CHARLIE

Golden Retriever Rescue of Wisconsin

Nick is seven years old, and Charlie is one. Nick is a boy and Charlie is a dog, which makes Charlie roughly the same age as Nick in human years. And in a lot of ways, they are similar. Nick runs in the house, and so does Charlie. Nick doesn't always listen to his mother, and neither does Charlie. Nick "accidently" gets in trouble, and so does Charlie. Nick loves to play outside, and so does Charlie—although neither of them will go out alone.

Nick has a four-year-old brother, Jacob. But there's only one Charlie, and so the battle over the dog rages on. When the three of them play together, it doesn't take long until at least one of them is complaining—and it's rarely Charlie. I suppose it's natural for an only dog to think he's human. I suppose it's also natural for him to think that he's not the smallest member of the pack because he outweighs the boys by more than a few pounds. But I'm pretty sure that it's not natural for a dog who weighs 85 pounds to jump in the lap of a 60-pound boy to be held. At least that doesn't feel natural to Nick. As Nick says, "I like it when he is the pillow, not me!"

Nick knows Charlie is a dog, but he usually treats Charlie better than he treats his brother. Of course, Charlie doesn't talk back or tell on Nick like Jake does. Jake gets very upset when Charlie is referred to as "Nick's Dog," but when Charlie gets in trouble, like the time he dug the 16-inch hole in the back yard, then Jake is happy to call him Nick's dog. (That's also when my husband and I alternately call him "Your" dog). But Charlie and Nick, too, have their battles. Charlie loves to carry things—any things, and it seems to make him happier when the things are Nicks. "Mom, Charlie has my shoe!" "Mom, Charlie has my baseball glove." "Mom, Charlie has my ball." Now Charlie, much like any sibling, won't drop the stolen item until told to do so by mom or dad. Nick yells, "Drop it!" Charlie just looks at him. So then Nick yells, "Charlie, Mom says drop it!" That doesn't work either.

Charlie isn't very good at sharing, which Nick can attest to, but he is excellent at tackling, which Jake can attest to. And, quite frankly, Mom and Dad are hoping that puppy-hood passes quickly. Having two boys and a dog is a lot of work. Now, in addition to four muddy shoe prints there are also four muddy paw prints.

I call this photograph "chalk trouble." Charlie's fur had mysteriously turned many colors. When I asked what happened, Nick said Charlie was too "plain-looking," and he thought he needed some color. When I scolded both boy and dog, here is the look I got from the two of them.

We adopted Charlie a year ago from the rescue organization that saved him and 5 golden retrievers from a puppymill.

—Lois Maurer

Dana Bourassa and Kodiak

KODIAK

Golden Retriever Rescue of Wisconsin

Kodiak's owner was a truck driver who took him traveling all over the country. Life was good for this young Golden until one spring day when he developed a noticeable limp in his right hind leg. Before long, Kodiak couldn't place any weight on this leg and was no longer able to get into the truck and travel. Initial tests done by the vet were inconclusive, and, unable to afford further vet expenses, Kodiak's owner left him at the clinic to be euthanized.

But instead of euthanizing him, the vet placed a call to GRROW, and so it was that Kodiak came into rescue and into my life. Kodiak was one of the most beautiful Goldens I had ever seen, not just in appearance, but also in something far greater that I was yet to discover.

Immediately, I took Kodiak to our vet to determine what was wrong, and my worst fear was confirmed: Kodiak had bone cancer. But he also had a robust love of life and, best of all, a winning attitude. I knew that, if any dog had a chance of beating this, it was Kodi. So without delay, we proceeded with surgery to amputate his hind right leg and start chemotherapy treatments. Through it all, Kodi never lost his happy smile and sense of fun. Despite the poking and prodding and lying on a table for hours with a needle in his vein, Kodi never once growled or lost his loving temperament. I knew then that I had discovered the other beautiful part of this Golden.

Sadly, though, the cancer spread to Kodi's lungs, and all that remained was to keep him comfortable as long as possible. Unbelievably, despite all he had gone through, Kodi was always his happy, playful self and one of the most loving and gentle dogs I have ever known. You couldn't look at Kodi and not feel happy. He was a clown, a companion, and a constant reminder that life is about loving. Perhaps the most poignant message is the one Kodiak offered to everyone he met: Face each day with joy, rejoice in the moment, and always have a smile.

A few months later, Kodiak lost his battle with cancer and crossed over the bridge. I'm sure he is now well and healthy, with all four legs, running and playing and bringing his special joy to all who are around him. Kodiak was love and joy, happiness and laughter. He has left a hole in my heart and it will be a long time before I stop grieving for him, but I know he's in a better place and no longer suffering. He touched my life and the lives of all who knew him in a very special way. If love could have saved him he would still be here.

—Dana Bourassa

Martha Garske and Gunner

GUNNER

Retrieve a Golden of Minnesota

The rescue group rescued Gunner from an abusive situation when he was two years old. When I went to meet Gunner, I found a beautiful, but extremely scrawny and sad looking golden retriever hunkering down in some evergreens, trying to hide. It was funny and heartbreaking at the same time. He tugged at my heart, it was love at first sight, and I adopted him.

Because he was abused, Gunner reacted unexpectedly to some things. Loud noises, sudden movements, sticks, and anything with wheels (go figure!) sent him running for cover. But gradually, he has learned that he's safe, and now these things no longer scare him as much.

Gunner does many things that make me laugh and here are just a few:

- He runs up and does a twirl in the air and lands before me whenever I call him.

- He looks a little goofy when his lips get caught on his crooked lower teeth.

- He snores at night, but it's a very quiet, peaceful, comforting snore.

- He often heaves a huge sigh as he lies down ("Life is SO rough.").

- He sometimes stalks inanimate objects on our walks.

- He and my cat Zeke lick each other's heads.

- He barks/growls at doorbells on TV.

Gunner is a wonderful, wonderful dog. He's my best friend, and I miss him when I'm at work during the day. He is always ready to do whatever I want to do. He is just a great friend and companion, and I love him dearly.

—Martha Garske

Nick, Kellie, Robby Sutherland and Ozzie

OZZIE

Retrieve a Golden of Minnesota

I never really considered myself a dog person. Not that I was against dogs, I just had never had a dog before, and I thought a dog wouldn't fit into our hectic lifestyle. You know, all the "doggy jobs" like baths, feeding, pooper scooping, brushing, vacuuming, more vacuuming…I just couldn't see how they would fit into my already crazy schedule.

However, my husband grew up with a golden retriever and, for the past 13 years, my family has been begging me for a dog (my husband for a golden retriever, specifically). Then, last summer, they turned me onto the rescue group's website, forcing me to read the profiles of every single golden retriever that was available for adoption. Finally, I realized "I must be missing something!"

Was I ever! Since we adopted Ozzie, I discovered what I've been missing! Ozzie has totally made our family complete and I can't imagine what we ever did without him. He's everything we hoped for and more. He follows us around everywhere we go, is totally trained, hardly ever barks and just is so darn cute you can't help but just want to hug him to pieces!

Ozzie has become such a real member of our family that when we have to leave him for any length of time, it really breaks our hearts! He's an awesome dog and we all love him to death. The goofiest thing that Ozzie does is "Melt" when someone pets him. If he's standing, he'll immediately sit and then lay and then roll over to get a belly rub!

Ozzie was one day away from being euthanized at the shelter when the rescue group saved him. I cannot even imagine putting a dog like this to sleep. He's like a gift and we are so grateful for him. It has been so much fun becoming a "dog person." I just never imagined I would ever feel like this!

—*Pam Sutherland*

Holly Renfrow and Koa

KOA

Retrieve a Golden of Minnesota

Growing up in Hawaii, I wanted a name for our newly adopted golden retriever that he could grow into, so I chose "King Koa," which means "brave and confident warrior." However, this was clearly not the dog before me.

Saved from a life of abuse and abandonment by the rescue group, Koa was terrified of everything and everyone. The slightest noise made him startle or run from the room. Feet posed a particular threat, causing him to cower in fear of being kicked. When I prepared his food bowl, he ran away and hid until I left the bowl unattended and then he would slink back into the kitchen to eat. Any sudden movement caused him to flatten against the floor.

Because I wasn't able to lure Koa with treats or physically help him into a sit or a down, I needed some training options and decided to try the "clicker method." Koa's trust skyrocketed from there! In one month's time, he learned 20 tricks and passed his Canine Good Citizen Test. Within 6 months, he was transformed into a different dog! We started training for agility during this time, and he blossomed with the challenge and the excitement of learning.

Koa has completed several agility titles, and now we perform agility demonstrations for the middle school. My husband took him through an AKC Junior Hunter course, and he works beautifully in the field flushing and retrieving pheasants, now excited about the loud noise of the gun. And every week we go to the assisted living community where

Koa provides pet therapy for the residents. He is constantly ready to work!

But best of all, Koa's sweet, loving spirit emerged. Although hints of the scars of abuse still remain, he now has the confidence to tackle new situations and to know that he has finally found his "forever home," which he shares with his new Golden rescued sister, Kaile.

—Holly Renfrow

Caleigh, Cameron, Jacob Kimberly and Buddy

BUDDY

Retrieve a Golden of Minnesota

Buddy was a stray that was rescued by the golden retriever rescue group. I decided that Buddy was the dog for us after reading the foster mom's note that, even with her 7 children, the dog tolerated everything. This was very important to me, because we had a 6-month-old baby at the time.

Buddy is the most gentle, loving animal I have ever known. He is kind and polite to the two cats that were already residing in the house. He tolerates his tail being pulled, his eyes poked, and even having his favorite toy being yanked from his mouth! If one of his toys is accidentally put away with the baby's toys, Buddy will gently and carefully sniff it out and take only his toy to play with, leaving the baby's alone!

Buddy is everybody's buddy. I work at home and love having Buddy constantly at my feet during the day. We are best buddies, although I think every member of the family feels the same about him. Cameron loves it when Buddy climbs into bed with him in the morning, and Caleigh walks with him and teaches him tricks. Jacob's first two words were Mama and Dadda, but he recently said his third word: Uddy! He just discovered he can feed Buddy food from his highchair, and Buddy sits so patiently waiting for that little hand to reach over with a piece of turkey! Buddy is also my husband's running companion every morning as they jog around the lake.

We have been so blessed to have this wonderful addition to our family. Buddy has made our house complete. My only hope is that he lives for a very, very long time. There will never be another dog like him.

—*Teresa Kimberly*

Jerry Campagnoli and Karma

KARMA

Retrieve a Golden of Minnesota

The golden retriever rescue group rescued Karma from the street, along with her 10 puppies. Only 1-year-old, she was debilitated by living on her own for weeks with pups, but she had a "Here I am!" attitude that could not be ignored. You could tell that, once given a little care, she would be beautiful again. Karma had that look in her eye that betokens a truly intelligent animal and, if she could have spoken, she would have said, "Take me, take me!" And we did. We adopted Karma from the golden retriever rescue group in the summer of 2000.

We discovered that, under all that neglect, was a simply gorgeous golden retriever, intelligent, funny, and soooo gentle and affectionate. I had read about the fabulous Golden personality, but could not have imagined what it was like to experience. Living with Karma is like getting a gift every single day.

Things that make us laugh? Her collection of woobies and the way she troops them out one at a time if you're not paying enough attention...the concept of a 74-pound lapdog who can't be convinced otherwise...her expression of total joy when presented with Frosty Paws...her crazy antics in the water...sound asleep on her back with all four paws in the air...or simply her exuberant love of life.

Karma is the perfect combination of an athletic "go get 'em" kind of dog and a cuddle bug of the first order. She can be demanding and capricious and she can be laid back and philosophical. In short, I guess she's a Golden, but are they all this fabulous?

—Roseann Campagnoli

Megan Johnson and Boone & Allie

BOONE

Retrieve a Golden of Minnesota

It became very obvious very soon after Boone's arrival in our home that he had a few little quirks, some anxieties that may or may not have been related to his early months spent in an Iowa puppymill. But from the very first minute when we met him, he was always exceptionally friendly. He's a very gentle and fun-loving dog and, like many golden retrievers, he's a serious attention seeker. He actively seeks out his human family and is always underfoot, never content to be just nearby, or outside if all of the rest of his family happens to be indoors.

But Boone is nervous, fearful of some common things like thunderstorms, vacuum cleaners, and almost all other loud noises, especially fireworks. My husband had hopes of Boone developing into a hunter but those hopes were dashed when it became painfully obvious just how gun-shy he was. Boone even runs in the other direction at the mere sight of the gun case as Mike prepares for his hunting outings. But some of his fears seem more unusual. He always gives trashcans a wide berth on our daily walks. The crossing arms at the nearby railroad crossing descended one day as we approached and Boone nearly jumped out of his skin!

I read some literature about the local pet therapy program and realized that, although Boone would never be a hunter, he certainly had the potential to bring joy to many more lives besides those of our family. I worked hard with Boone training him at home to meet the criteria of the Canine Good Citizen exam, a requirement for becoming a pet therapy dog. He was an amazingly quick study, so easy to train and so eager to please. At the tender age of 18 months, he passed his exam. In a crowded room full of other dogs, he was focused, confident, and not one bit nervous or anxious. He passed with flying colors on his first try!

Since that time, Boone and I have made numerous visits to hospitals, nursing homes, and schools, and it is beyond heartwarming to watch the joy this dog brings to others. This sometimes anxious, nervous dog can go to the local children's museum on a crowded Saturday afternoon and have a wagging tail and a cold nose for each child that approaches him. He's very gentle at the nursing home. The smiles of the elderly as they reminisce about dogs in their past while they cradle Boone's head in their lap is enough to bring tears to any eye.

Boone truly seems to be a study in contrasts. He has his little quirks and anxieties, but he also seems to be aware of his calling. He seems to know that, when his bandanna is placed around his neck, he's working and he seems to know exactly what that work is.

—Ellen Johnson

James and Barbara Hart & Angel

ANGEL

Golden Retriever Rescue of Wisconsin

I first saw Angel when the rescue group held a "Meet and Greet" at a local pet store. She was only about 4 months old at the time, a cute, playful little puppy. I really wanted to take her home with me right then, but was told that, because of her health, she wasn't ready for adoption yet. A month went by, and we assumed that surely someone must have already adopted this sweet little puppy. The rescue group returned for another "Meet & Greet" and Angel was there again. This time, we submitted an application, hoping that we would be given the chance to adopt her. Everything moved along very quickly after that.

We've had Angel for about a week now, and she is quickly becoming part of the family. She has such a cute face and she can be very endearing when she snuggles up next to you, puts her head on your arm or leg and goes to sleep. She won the human part of the family over right away. I'm not sure that our other two Goldens felt there was a need for a third dog, but they have tolerated her well and seem to accept her a little more every day. Angel and our cat have also had to work out the ground rules. Angel is quite fascinated with the cat, though sometimes she has gotten a bit too curious and has received a few well-placed taps on the nose.

It's been a long time, almost seven years, since we've had a puppy at our house. We had forgotten the level of energy and enthusiasm a puppy can bring. Angel loves to run around the yard chasing bugs and can always seem to find something that interests her. There is a dog park near our home, and Angel loves to go there to run and play with the other dogs. A shallow river runs through the park, and Angel has proven to be quite a water bug. She loves to bound through the water. Her youthful enthusiasm does get the better of her sometimes, and I believe she would keep going until she drops if we would let her.

As sweet as she usually is, there are times when I think she should have been named Devil rather than Angel. She barks when she's frustrated, appears to have a shoe fetish, sometimes nips at our heels, and will occasionally shred papers. All in all, however, Angel is a delight. She's loving, playful, and a most welcome addition to our family.

When she was only 4 weeks old, Angel was sold by a puppymill to a woman who surrendered her to the rescue group. Weighing only 3 pounds, Angel had extensive bladder and kidney problems, which caused her to be incontinent. Although surgery corrected the incontinence, both her kidneys are damaged from a severe infection early in life. We know Angel's health is uncertain and that there are no guarantees, but we will make the most of whatever time we have with her.

—Barbara Hart

Lee and Scott Gregory & Bailey

BAILEY

Old Gold Senior Dog Rescue Louisiana

As soon as my husband and I bought our first house, we began searching for a Golden to adopt. We spent hours on the Internet looking at rescued Goldens before we found Bailey. When we saw his picture and read his story, we fell in love with him and, a few days later, drove six hours to pick him up.

Bailey had been lost out in the country for a long time before he was found and turned over to the golden retriever rescue group. He's a big Golden, but he'd lost so much weight that every bone in his body was sticking out. He was infested with fleas and ticks and suffering from heartworms and intestinal parasites. And he was also very scared. When he finally arrived home with us, he was still underweight and very nervous.

It didn't take him long, however, to fit right into our family. Over the next few weeks he gradually put on weight and his nervousness subsided. We could actually see him becoming happy! Bailey's favorite time is summer when we can take him to the lake. We have to be dressed for swimming when we take him to the water, because he'll go out as far as he can while still standing on the lake bottom.

Bailey absolutely loves to ride in the car. He can be upstairs on the other side of the house, but when I pick up the car keys he comes galloping to the back door to be sure he doesn't miss out on a car ride! Just before we got Bailey we found a kitten. At first we wondered how this huge dog would react to the tiny kitten, but Bailey has never been anything but gentle with her, and now the two are great friends. Each night, they both jump up on our bed. For a while they'll play together and then when they settle down, the cat will give Bailey a bath before they finally fall asleep.

We've often wondered how Bailey came to be lost in the country and what happened to him in his previous life. He is the most loving, gentle dog I've ever known. That the rescue group saved him and entrusted him to us is a gift we can never repay.

—Lee Gregory

Laura Watrous and Ben

BEN

Triad Golden Retriever Rescue

Ben was a tragic victim of neglect. He was turned into the animal shelter with seven other dogs in the Allegheny mountain area of North Carolina and they were in such bad shape they all died, except Ben. He was very thin, covered with mange and almost blind from bilateral entropy of the eyelids. There was emotional neglect as well. Ben was incredibly shy and terrified to step foot into a house, fearful of getting into cars and walking on a leash. Thankfully, the golden retriever rescue group found him at the shelter and saved him.

I was still grieving the loss of my beloved greyhound Kodak who had died from bone cancer 4 months earlier when I came across Ben's story on the Internet. He was described as "a young *special needs* Golden who needs someone to give him love, training and help him build up his confidence." I looked at the photo of Ben on the screen and knew right then we would soon be family.

Thinking back to the moment we first met still brings tears to my eyes. I knelt down in the grass and called his name and he came to me and looked me in the eyes like he had known me all along. From the first moment he trusted me, and it was then I knew I could help him heal.

The first few months were a real challenge as Ben adjusted to his new life. The rescue group had already taken care of his eye surgery and cured his mange, but his emotional fears lingered. Every new experience he encountered with trepidation. It was obvious Ben had never known the fun things in dog life like sleeping on the bed, going for walks, swimming in the ocean, and chasing the ball. But he loved me more than anything, and little by little he began to come out of his shell.

Nowadays we can't keep Ben out of the water at the beach. He loves chasing seagulls and will swim way out to try to catch them! Going for walks is one of his favorite things and he becomes a madman when he sees his leash or hears the word "walk." He even begins each walk by taking the leash into his mouth and leading us down the driveway. Today, Ben will chase a ball and pounce on it in joyful glee. I get so excited just watching him. He has blossomed into a beautiful, confident Golden and it's hard to believe this is the same dog that was afraid of everything.

Ben has been with us for two years now. He warms the heart of everyone he meets and is an absolute joy to have around. Everyday he proves to us how patience will be rewarded and now we can't imagine our lives without Ben. We feel so incredibly lucky to have found him and he feels the same way towards us. Ben was given a second chance at life and we are blessed to witness his gratitude every day!

—*Laura Watrous*

Paula and Greg Bulkley & Paddington

PADDINGTON

Inland Empire Golden Retriever Rescue

The first time we saw Paddington was on TV as a news camera panned a very busy Pet Adoption Festival at the local mall. In the middle of it all was a three-legged Golden Retriever. Out of curiosity, we went to see him. We weren't looking for another dog, we already had one Golden, and he was doing just fine. Then we met Paddington.

There was a great deal of interest in Paddington's surgery, but no interest in adopting him. With staples and sutures securing the wound from his recently removed leg, Paddington was unsure of his footing on the tiles at the mall, so we carried him outside to the grass. My wife cradled Paddington's face in her hands, and her heart opened up to his beautiful brown eyes. When it was time to carry him back inside, my wife guided my hands, so I wouldn't hurt his incision. He was pure trust. He didn't whimper, cry or squirm. He's a large dog, but it was obvious from the start that most of his weight comes from a huge Golden Retriever heart. We knew then that Paddington was meant to come home with us.

Paddington's leg was broken at three months and not removed until he was just over a year old. He grew up with an unusable left rear leg, so he needed to learn how to move all over again. And this being his third home in a very short time added to his confusion. When presented with a challenge, he would sometimes lie down and give up, or shy away. Each day, now, he expands his boundaries and abilities on three legs. Tiles are no longer daunting, long staircases are less of an obstacle, running in winter snow was just plain exhilarating, and learning to swim is the latest summer adventure. Seamus (our other Golden) has taken on the responsibility of being a mentor and is the rock Paddington turns to when he is unsure. The first glimpse of a ceiling fan was scary, until he saw Seamus simply stretch out to enjoy the breeze. Open staircases were insurmountable until Seamus came back down, licked his muzzle and led the way back up. Paddington knows exactly where to look when he needs a little encouragement, his big brother.

Every time we see a change in Paddington, there is a change in us. He is building up the muscles and balance he needs to maneuver on three legs, and the progress is phenomenal. It's easy for us to forget he is missing a leg. His spirit is pure Golden Retriever and so is his personality. We truly feel we were drawn to the mall that day for a reason. We've given Paddington a loving home, but he is giving us so much more in return.

—*Greg Bulkley*

Trish Herrera and Rosie

ROSIE

Golden Beginnings

After the wake of September 11, I felt an incredible need to somehow help someone or do something. I asked the universe, "What can I do to help?" I considered adopting a child or perhaps going to NYC to help clean up the debris. I've always made my life and environment about peace of mind and love, and I have lots of friends who respect animals and nature. But now I felt so sad and useless and in need of a direction. I wanted life around me. I knew that would be the only way to fill my home back up with joy.

I have a 14-year-old Golden Retriever mix named Tom that I adore, and my Mother suggested I adopt another dog. So I adopted 4-year-old Rosie from the rescue group. A stray who had been treated for heartworms, Rosie was very fearful, usually trying to hide under my dining room table. She was afraid of loud noises and men who carried things. Tom and I worked very hard to bring Rosie out of her fear and, little by little, she began to trust all of us and even greet men at the door.

Soon after I adopted Rosie, a veterinarian examination revealed she had severe hip dysplasia and needed surgery on both hips. I began to cry, knowing this was going to be painful for her and expensive for me, five thousand dollars expensive to be exact. How could I afford this? My work as a hairdresser makes a good living, but I didn't have enough money to pay for these surgeries. I didn't know what to do so I called Golden Beginnings and they came up with an idea. A fundraiser! With the help of Golden Beginnings and my family and friends, we raised the money for Rosie's surgeries! My lucky Rose. Rosie and I set a precedent by creating a new fund for Golden Beginnings that would help newly adopted dogs with special needs like hers. The fund was appropriately named the Rosie Fund.

A lot has happened since we found our little caramel girl. Rosie has had 3 surgeries so far, one ACL surgery which was very successful and two hip replacements which, unfortunately, did not work for Rosie. She didn't receive the youthful hips I had prayed for her, and we were both exhausted. I decided, "Enough hospitals and doctors for awhile." Now we spend our time healing and hoping her hips will not give her pain as she grows older. Rosie has changed us all with her bravery, and somehow I believe there is a higher purpose for what she has endured.

I call her my "Green Bean" and she cocks her head at me. She is so full of love and so willing to enjoy her new life. She looks after the failing Tom who is having a happy end of his life with his new friend. Rosie is secure and happy and knows she has found her forever home with Tom and me. So what happened when I asked the universe to allow me to help after 9/11? I was given the path of helping a little Golden doggie with big beautiful eyes. Ask and you will receive a Rose.

—*Trish Herrera*

Mike McHann and Goldie

GOLDIE

Tennessee Valley Golden Retriever Rescue

Remember the cartoon character Goofy? Well, kinda goofy is the best way I can think of to describe Goldie. I guess it's because she's so long and lanky, a tad clumsy, coordination just a little lacking, always bumping into things, and slipping and sliding on the tile floor, especially when she's taking those corners at 90 miles an hour. Adding to the somewhat "goofy perception" is her great big head and the long, unruly tufts of hair sticking out in all directions all over her body. Goldie is good-natured and always seems to be having a good time.

When we first got Goldie, she had a hard time keeping her balance on car rides because of those long legs, so she felt safest lying flat in the back seat. Not anymore! She figured out how to keep her balance and now she always has her head out the window, ears flying in the wind! Goldie loves to chase the many squirrels in our yard; she exits the back door slowly, as if she's stalking, then takes off like a flash as soon as she spots one. Of course, she never actually catches a squirrel, but she seems to have fun trying! More than anything, Goldie loves to be petted. I have no doubt she would stand for hours with her head at the end of a moving hand, eyes closed with pleasure. In fact, sometimes I get distracted reading the newspaper during a petting session and my hand stops moving, at which point she begins to move her head back and forth, in essence "petting herself!" Goldie is a wonderful companion to our aging Golden Leo, always leaving a bit of food behind in her bowl for him to finish off and never rushing him through the doorways. She seems to understand his slowness and respect his seniority, for which Leo is very appreciative.

Goldie is a wonderful dog, carefree and happy, gentle and loving, mischievous and playful; this despite the neglect and suffering she has endured. In the dead of winter, Goldie's owner moved away and abandoned her to fend for herself. For the next two years, she waited for his return, living under the porches of houses and surviving on scraps tossed her way. Finally, when a leg injury temporarily crippled her, Goldie was taken to the animal shelter by a neighbor who recounted her story on the release form. The rescue group saved her from the shelter and successfully treated her leg injury, in the process discovering an old leg fracture, the small bullet still imbedded in the bone.

Regular visitors to the group's website, my wife Margie and I were horrified to read Goldie's story and immediately made arrangements to adopt her. That was 6 months ago and this big, beautiful goofy girl with the painful past now has a happy new life with us. We love our silly girl and she loves us.

—*Mike McHann*

Karin Jessen and Koby

KOBY

Tennessee Valley Golden Retriever Rescue

Scared, thin, dirty, matted, and full of worms, Koby was rescued from the local shelter by the golden retriever rescue organization. As a volunteer, I picked him up from the shelter and delivered him to the kennels where he was to be boarded due to lack of foster homes. I had 3 dogs of my own, one of them very sick, so I didn't feel like I could foster another dog at the time.

The following weekend, the group held an Adoptathon to showcase our adoptable golden retrievers, and I volunteered to be Koby's chaperone for the day. We spent the day meeting potential parents, and he was such a gentleman that I couldn't imagine anyone not loving this dog! At the end of the day, I couldn't bear to return him to the kennels, so I took him home with me. In the days to come, Koby proved to be a sweet, gentle, loving soul. He never barked, but he never wagged his tail, he didn't play with my dogs, and he certainly didn't know what toys were. He hardly ate, he just lay in the corner, very quiet and out of the way.

Over the next few months, several families considered Koby, but he was never chosen. Finally, he was adopted by a family, but returned 2 days later because they "changed their minds." When this family brought him back, Koby came over and sat next to me and looked up at me with his big brown eyes and told me he was home! How could I not keep this dog? Well, Koby adopted us and we really had no choice, he had found his forever home and that was the way it was going to be!

We've had Koby for almost a year now. It took him 6 months to learn how to be a happy dog. He learned how to wag his tail, how to play with his sisters, how to squeak toys and generally how to be a dog again. He learned how to fetch a ball, how to play chase and be chased, he even learned how to bark! Koby has truly adapted to the soft life and even prefers to be inside now, rather than outside. He also knows that if he's the first one upstairs at night, then he gets first choice of beds, and that's the best thing of all!

—*Karin Jessen*

Janie Heatherly and Moses & Madison

MOSES & MADISON

Tennessee Valley Golden Retriever Rescue

This is a story about two of my very best friends. Last fall, we adopted 8 yo Moses and 10 yo Madison from the Tennessee Valley Golden Retriever Rescue. Moses had been saved from death at the animal shelter and Madison had been surrendered by her owner who had developed severe health problems. We've had them almost a year now and feel as though they have always been a part of our lives.

These Golden babies have so much to offer. I am so very proud of them and love sharing them with others. Moses and Madison are both certified therapy dogs and they visit nursing homes and a home for mentally challenged adults. It's so wonderful to see the joy they bring to the residents of these facilities.

Recently, my husband and I received special permission to take the M&M team into the Tennessee Prison for Women where we do prison ministry. This is a first in Tennessee prisons and a very great honor for Moses and Madison! The M&M team were so well received by the girls in the prison, it's a miracle they had any fur left after all the petting and love they got. The girls and the dogs exchanged so much love it was a wonderful sight to see. The M&M team knew exactly what to do like they had been there many times. The girls were very curious about the dogs' background and, proud mom that I am, I love telling their story. The girls received unconditional love they don't always get from society. They share a common bond with Moses and Madison; they have been rejected, unloved and literally thrown away.

We are so blessed by these Golden friends; I thank God for bringing them into our lives. Our lives, and the lives of so many others, are more Golden because of Moses and Madison.

—Janie Heatherly

Angel Mahoney and Dillon

DILLON

Tennessee Valley Golden Retriever Rescue

One of my favorite forms of affection would have to be hugging. How perfect for me that I have a dog that feels the same way. Each evening when I return from work, Dillon greets me by standing up and hugging me, burying his head against me. It's as if he's saying, "Oh thank you for coming back to me!"

Dillon LOVES to take me for walks. He can hardly contain himself when he sees the leash. He actually grabs one end of it and sprints to the front door. Once we're outside, he's pulling me along behind him. We do have to stay out of the street because Dillon will try to get into the cars of people driving by. If he ever gets out and is roaming free in the neighborhood, all I have to do is drive down the road and he comes running towards the car. I just open up and let him in.

I know when he needs to go out in the morning because his nose is resting on the mattress by my bed. He just stands next to the bed, with his head resting on the bed, looking at me. He does the same thing with my lap if I'm watching television. He just rests his head there on my lap for me to pet him. I'm not allowed to stop once I start either. If I stop petting him, he'll nudge his nose back under my arm.

Dillon Mahoney spent the first two years of his life outside and all alone in a 5x8 foot cage. Eventually, his owners were persuaded to surrender him to the golden retriever rescue group, where he spent the next 6 months being socialized to "regular dog life" and being cured of his heartworms. It's been great to see him grow healthier and develop since I adopted him. He's not as scared of going into rooms or going up and down stairs as he was in the beginning. I still have to walk out-side with him to go to the bathroom. If he doesn't see me at least standing in the doorway of the back yard, he won't go outside. I don't mind, he's just my little boy, and I don't know what I would do with-out him! It's an incredible feeling to have someone like him to love and to truly feel him love me back.

—*Angel Mahoney*

Sarah Houser and Fletcher

FLETCHER

Tennessee Valley Golden Retriever Rescue

When Fletcher's original family realized he had severe hip dysplasia, they put him in the newspaper "free to good home" and the rescue group took him in. A handsome, blonde 2-year-old golden retriever, Fletcher had to struggle to get up and was constantly in pain. Surgery was done on his worst hip to implant a prosthesis, and now Fletcher gets around just fine. Eventually, he may need the second hip surgery, but the vet says it's possible he'll do just fine without it.

When I met Fletcher at the Adoptathon last year, it was love at first sight. I'm a single woman and Mother to 3-year-old Golden fur baby Crockett, and I'd never considered getting a second dog. I can't explain it, but I knew instantly that Fletcher was meant for Crockett and me and so I adopted him.

Crockett is my mild-mannered, prim and proper dog, and Fletcher is my WILD MAN. Whenever there's trouble, I always know who the culprit is. The first couple of months, Fletch was only into minor trouble; getting bubble gum tangled in his coat, climbing into the bathtub as I was drawing water for a bath, and surfing the countertops. I tried my best to reprimand him, but Fletch is so darn cute that it's hard to be stern with him. Crockett justs sits on the sidelines and rolls his eyes.

We were into month two when it happened. I awoke one morning to find Fletch vomiting, and tests at the vet clinic confirmed he had a blockage. During the emergency exploratory surgery, the vet removed plastic, sticks, rocks, and a sock! For 48 hours it was touch and go, but Fletch pulled through with flying colors.

Crockett and Fletcher and I are inseparable. I take them everywhere with me, and I know I just have to pay close attention to Fletch to help him stay out of trouble. I'm a guidance counselor; my office walls are decorated with pictures of Fletcher and Crockett, and I think that, in their own way, Fletch and Crockett bring comfort to my students.

I don't know what I would do without Fletcher and Crockett. They mean everything to me and they are a part of everything I do. I'm so grateful to TVGRR for saving Fletcher; I can't imagine what my life would be like without him.

—*Sarah Houser*

Debi Mitchell and Haylee Anna

HAYLEE ANNA

Tennessee Valley Golden Retriever Rescue

The first time I saw little 5-month-old Haylee was when she bolted into the crowded Vet's waiting room, all legs and energy, bypassed everyone else and made a beeline straight for MY lap. It was as if she "picked me" out of everyone else in the room. From that moment, I felt a strange and wonderful connection with Haylee Anna. Our rescue group had saved Haylee from the shelter, and my husband and I volunteered to foster her until she was adopted. But within a week we were signing adoption papers!

Haylee is my "heart dog." We are so connected that we seem to know what the other is thinking. She has been a guardian angel for all the foster Goldens that have come through my house over the years, carefully caring for each and everyone. She was a wonderful sister to our beloved rescue Cody Monroe, who died last year, and she continues to be a good sister to Alex, our latest spoiled rotten adoptee.

Haylee loves the water and enjoys her trips out on the lake in our pontoon boat. She stands in the front of the boat, ears flapping in the wind, watching the ducks and geese pass by. Sometimes I think she looks like "The Flying Nun" from the old TV series! Another one of Haylee's favorite pastimes is "lizard hunting!" Haylee is quite the huntress and can concentrate and remain completely still in order to achieve her goal. It's rare that she actually hurts anything unless it's so small that she can't help it; there have been occasions when she brought me a dead or injured lizard, only to look at me as if she wanted me to make it all better.

A funny story about Haylee's hunting instincts comes to mind. One day as I approached Haylee in the backyard, I noticed that she had a very strange look on her face. As I came closer, I was convinced she was hiding something from me. I put my hand under her mouth and told her to "drop it." At first, she resisted, but then she gingerly spit it out in my hand. This had happened many times before and I would never know exactly what I would be left holding, but this time I was shocked! Very carefully, she placed a beautiful Yellow Finch into my hand. It was only there for a split second before it flew off home. This was the last thing I expected. Not only did Haylee catch that bird, but also she didn't harm it while catching it. I then understood that strange look on her face; the tiny finch was apparently moving around in her mouth and Haylee was a little unsure as to what to do with it. I remember laughing about it for the rest of the day. To this day, I have not found anyone else whose dog was able to catch a Yellow Finch, unharmed! What talent my little girl has!

Haylee Anna is a true fur angel. She has been with me for 5 years now, and her kindness and gentleness have endeared her to me for a lifetime.

—Debi Mitchell

Chandler Rudd and Lucy

LUCY

Yankee Golden Retriever Rescue

On one of the coldest winter days of 1997, a golden retriever puppy was found in a downtown dumpster and taken to a vet clinic, where it was discovered she was paralyzed from the "waist down" from a birth defect or injury. The pup was accepted by the golden retriever rescue group and admitted into their program, the goal being to rehabilitate her in preparation for adoption. This resulted in the amputation of her useless hind leg, enabling her to use her remaining hind leg to run, but not to walk. During these months of rehabilitation, the young Golden lived at the clinic, but eventually, my wife and I volunteered to foster her until she was adopted. It would only be temporary, I wouldn't become attached to Lucy, and I would consider her a work in progress, a job, so to speak.

One night, while Lucy was sleeping on the couch, I watched her as she dreamed. Her eyes, although closed, moved as she watched something in her dreamworld. Her legs moved rhythmically as she chased it. I wondered if she was still handicapped in her dreams, or if she could run as she had never done. I moved closer to her, studying her face, looking at the perfection in her features and wondered why something so beautiful, so innocent, could be so imperfect. As I drew even closer, Lucy must have sensed my presence. Her eyes opened a little, and when she saw me so near, they opened wide in surprise. Then something happened that changed everything. She recognized me. Her eyes softened, and she leaned closer to me and gently licked my face. This one act went straight to my heart. I knew then that I was totally in love

OUACHITA TECHNICAL COLLEGE

with this little girl and that we would never part. She had found her "forever home."

My wife and I realized that Lucy, with her disability and her wonderful personality, could help handicapped children overcome the obstacles in their journey towards rehabilitation. We felt that Lucy was put on this earth for a purpose. She had come a long way and fought incredible odds just to get this far. Now we had a new "job," to help Lucy help others. It took almost a year, but now Lucy is a certified therapy dog and works with a local Rehabilitation Hospital, every week seeing as many as 30 patients.

We want everyone to know that Lucy leads a pretty normal life. Like any other Golden, she swims and spends hours retrieving her tennis balls. She travels with us wherever we go. She rides in a modified jogging stroller when we go on our walks, but she gets down and plays with the other dogs from time to time. She has become something of a celebrity, her story being told in magazines, Internet sites, and on public television. We're supported by a wonderful group of people who have stuck with us through everything, and it's that support that made us realize we have a very special Golden.

—Chandler Rudd

Cody and Julie Callaway and Thunder

THUNDER

Gold Ribbon Rescue

His owners surrendered Thunder to the golden retriever rescue group when he was 2 years old because they said they didn't have time for him. I'll never understand how they could relinquish such a wonderful dog, but I'm glad that they did! Otherwise, my husband and I would have missed the joy of knowing and loving this sweet, gentle, happy Golden.

As soon as we adopted Thunder, he fit right into our household as if he'd always been here. He quickly became the favorite of all our friends and family because he loved people, especially children, and greeted everyone with a big smile and wagging tail. Yet I believe that I was Thunder's very favorite person. Every night he settled in and slept by my side of the bed, and mornings he greeted me with a big grin and happy, wagging tail. We were special to each other.

Thunder was everything you'd ever want in a dog...playful, yet laid back in the house...happy and good with everyone he met...frisky when we walked on cool windy days...my best friend when I needed a shoulder...one of the most beautiful Goldens I've ever seen. He'd sleep on our bed when we were gone and then quickly jump down when he heard us coming. Sometimes we'd quietly sneak in to catch him in the act. Everyone loved Thunder.

After two short years, Thunder became ill and was taken from me much too early. I miss him every day. I miss him sleeping by my side of the bed every night, the way he looked out the window as I drove away, his excitement at the slightest jingling of his leash, and how he was constantly underfoot. I regret that my son will not be able to grow up with him; Thunder died just a few months after my son was born.

If there's one thing I've learned from losing Thunder, it's that you never take for granted every precious moment you have with your loyal friend. I'm thankful to Gold Ribbon Rescue for bringing him into my life.

—Julie Calloway

Rue Chagoll and Sydney

SYDNEY

Golden Retriever Rescue of Central New York

What a horrible shock it was when our beloved Sydney passed away. One day he romped with our other Goldens, enthusiastically greeted visitors, and was his typical vocal self at feeding time. Five days later he was gone. Initially I was filled with grief, but a feeling of tranquility began to envelop me as the sad day wore on, and I wondered why. We'd just lost one of the most wonderful dogs I'd ever known. Had I become conditioned to the dreadful experience of losing a treasured Golden friend? Shuddering at that notion, I became angry with myself for not feeling more tormented.

Sydney came to us through Golden Retriever Rescue of Central NY three years ago at age 9½, after prior owners were referred by a vet who'd refused to euthanize him for being a "high maintenance" dog. He came to our home for fostering—grossly overweight, nearly hairless, covered with scabs, exuding the horrible odor of a massive skin infection. A friend burst into tears at first sight of him. He was miserable, but managed a wag of the tail when I bent to greet him. I think it was right then we decided Sydney was in his "forever" home—whether it be for a week or a year, however long he had left. I couldn't bear the thought of risking him to so much as another day of neglect. With surgery to remove an ugly skin tumor, treatment for hypothyroidism, and a good diet and exercise, Syd began a miraculous rebound. For probably the first time in his life he began to grow feathers on his tail.

Syd entered the daily rotation of dogs I take to the office. Bounding into the car at every opportunity, he'd sit the entire trip in regal pose as though evaluating my performance as his personal chauffeur. In summer we took him to the lake with our other dogs, and he began to catch on to the idea that water is a natural place for a Golden to be. Syd made friends wherever he went, refusing to be ignored and sporting the best nose in our pack for discovering a pocket with treats. From the pathetic figure we first met, never before permitted for other than short periods into a home, emerged a happy Golden whose spirit and zest for life belied his age. At Fun Day '98 Syd earned his Canine Good Citizen certificate and I walked him proudly in the Rescue Parade. He appeared at GRRCNY's public events, and went on many home visits to demonstrate first hand the joy to be experienced in having a senior Golden. Sydney became an ambassador not just for rescue, but also for his breed. Happy days.

So why now wasn't I more distraught over Syd's passing? Gradually, it began to dawn on me. A good friend had frequently told Syd, "You're the luckiest dog in the world." I was always quick to retort that no, it was we who were lucky to be blessed with his companionship. But on reflection I know she was right, too. From the time he arrived, we treated him though each day might be his last. We spent extra effort to help him "catch up" on life as a beloved and treasured member of our family.

It pains me to see wonderful dogs exiled to the deep background of peoples' lives. So many are acquired with not so much forethought as an article of furniture, and often disposed of with the same casual attitude. I hold little hope for that kind, believing you can't teach what should be understood by default. But it's for the rest of us, who love and want the very best for our dogs—but often find ourselves distracted with other aspects of our busy lives—that I share our experience with Sydney. We made the most of our time with him and he paid us back in spades, bestowing a basketful of happy memories. I'm certain now that's why, though my heart still aches, I was able to accept his passing with but few regrets.

I'll always regret Syd spent so much of his life deprived of the things he deserved, and that the three years we had with him couldn't have been four, or five, or fifteen. But I've found comfort in believing he harbored no regrets whatsoever, and from his perspective we'd made every shared day count. He basked in our care and companionship—celebrating every day in our family while dismissing his past—and departed this life a happy and fulfilled dog. Comforted in that, I can tuck dear Sydney into my heart for eternity, letting go with a smile, and continue forth honoring the needs of the other deserving Goldens in my life. Syd will be looking on with tail-wags of approval.

—Rue Chagoll

Tina Fisher and Taylor

TAYLOR

Gold Ribbon Rescue

Our sweet Taylor came into our lives four years ago when we adopted her from the Gold Ribbon Rescue. Never in a million years did I imagine I'd become so crazy about a dog that I would send her postcards when I go on vacation, call her on the phone, serve birthday cakes covered with dog bones, or sing "You are So Beautiful to Me!" (and mean it!).

Taylor is sweet, lovable, endearing, friendly, trusting, the best! She's my best friend and constant companion. A real treat for us is going for car rides with all the windows down, her ears blowing in the breeze while I'm honking and waving to all the Goldens and their owners walking along the road. Taylor even fetches the morning newspaper from the driveway for me, brings it inside, prances proudly around and then "plops" it in my lap! Her favorite trick is to balance a dog bone on her nose, then jump up and catch it in her mouth.

I think Taylor is absolutely the best in every way. The only thing I would change if I could is that she would live as long as I do!

—*Tina Fisher*

Mary Hannington and Memphis

MEMPHIS

Tennessee Valley Golden Retriever Rescue

I needed him as much as he needed me. He was recovering from heart-worms and the loss of the only home he'd ever known. I needed to fill the empty space left by the loss of my much beloved Golden, the only dog I had ever raised from a puppy. I wasn't yet ready to start all over with a new puppy, so when I came across a dark Golden with deep brown eyes on a rescue website, my spouse and I made the 750-mile trip to Memphis, Tennessee to meet him.

This quiet adult dog that seemed such a perfect fit was, in fact, an untrained maniac in disguise. At first, he was skittish and preferred staying outside under the deck. Then he became destructive and aggressive with toys; he even developed the obsessive-compulsive behavior of circling with his tail in his mouth. After months of daily training and lots of patience and love, Memphis has become an atten-tive pupil. He's been a part of the family for two years now, and in that time he has not only learned obedience and utility, but also how to love and trust his humans. At almost six years old he is still the puppy I didn't think I was ready for, but that's okay. I love him just the way he is.

—*Mary Hannington*

John Randall and Nutmeg & Cinnamon

NUTMEG

Tennessee Valley Golden Retriever Rescue

Nutmeg got a rocky start in life. Labeled as overly aggressive by her original owners, she was surrendered to the golden retriever rescue group and came to our home as a foster dog where we welcomed her with open arms and lots of love. In new surroundings, the transformation was immediate and complete. Not only did she not display any type of aggression, but she got along famously with our other Golden, Cinnamon, and was friendly to everyone she met. It didn't take long for us to fall in love with Nutmeg and make her a permanent part of our family. What we didn't realize was that Nutmeg would become a hero.

Nutmeg qualifies as a 'hero' on two levels, by being both a therapy dog and a search and rescue dog. Based on her obedience training and her Golden personality, she was selected for training as a "Specialty Command Therapy Dog" for utilization in the St. Mary's Hospital Rehabilitation Center. Serving faithfully one day each week, her invaluable contribution to the lives of stroke and brain injury patients has been impressive and undeniable. Not only does she facilitate improved speech and motor skills, but her ability to alleviate a patient's depression is evident by the instantaneous and dramatic changes in the patient's countenance as soon as Nutmeg steps paw into the room. Nominated by St Mary's, Nutmeg became the winner of this year's Golden Rescue And Community Excellence (GRACE) award, which recognizes her role in improving human health, independence, and quality of life.

In her other role, Nutmeg serves with her "sister" Cinnamon as a member of the Knoxville Volunteer Rescue Squad. After extensive training in agility, Trailing/Tracking and AirScent/Wilderness Search & Rescue, Nutmeg has successfully trailed three missing persons: a young child, an Alzheimer's patient, and a man lost in the woods. Nutmeg's efforts in saving, preserving and improving human life are a matter of public record, as is her recognition as a true "Hero" by her induction into the Tennessee Animal Hall of Fame.

When we put on their working vests for rescue or therapy visits, Nutmeg and Cinnamon know it's time to work and it changes their personalities. They're all business at that point in time. Nutmeg is a fantastic dog. We are so fortunate to have been able to adopt her and that she's accomplished such wonderful things for those in her community.

—John Randall

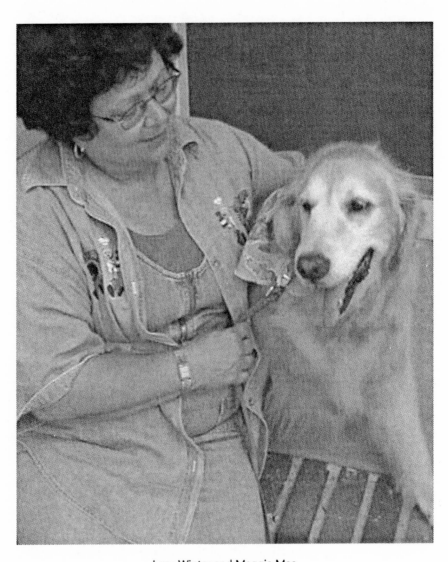

Lana Winter and Maggie Mae

MAGGIE MAE

Love A Golden

Labor Day Weekend 2001, I headed out to Goldstock with my rescued Goldens Briar, Patch and Truman. I shared a quiet cabin with my friend and her 3 foster dogs, which included Maggie Mae, a big, old, beautiful, white-faced, sexy broad who was saved from a kill shelter by the rescue group. During the weekend, Maggie Mae escaped the cabin on more than one occasion to wander through camp, take in the sights and look for treats. She swam in the lake, rolled in the sand and soaked up life.

Monday morning, bags packed, I prepared to leave for home. Subaru doors open, three Goldens aboard, and there's that blond broad trying to climb into the side door! Maggie Mae was determined and wouldn't take no for an answer! "Oh well, what's one more!" and I gave her a final boost and the five of us are "*on the road again.*"

That was a year ago, and it's hard to imagine what life would be like without Maggie Mae. She has created her own notch in my heart. Maggie Mae is the perfect Golden with impeccable house manners. She still opens storm doors (now the others have learned that if they stand very close to Maggie they can escape into the backyard as well!) and will sprawl across the floor if asked to do something she has no intention of doing, hooking her paws around your legs and smiling at the same time. Except for her white face, you wouldn't know she was a senior of 11 or more. She can run with the best of them, have a good roll in the grass and be first at the door to get a cookie or a car ride (which is a feat because she has to throw her left front leg to the side when she walks or runs due to a break that was never set).

Maggie attends socialization classes every week where she has a man friend, a black Shepard named Harmon. She has a monthly "day of beauty" at the dog salon where she's pampered and bathed. There are those great visits to a local nursing home, and we also started a program with the Corrections Department where Maggie visits teenage boys who pamper her with care while they learn responsibility, grooming, and training. I can't think of a better ambassador than Maggie Mae to teach these boys about love.

I know in my heart that I won't have the years with Maggie that I would like, but I intend to enjoy every moment we do have together, every single moment. Do I love this big beautiful blond? Indeed I do. "Wake up Maggie your Mom has something to say to you."

—Lana Winter

Nan Schramm and Hope

HOPE

Golden Retriever Rescue Operated with Love Statewide, Inc.

My husband and I adopted our 8-week-old female Golden from an incredible rescue group in upstate New York. She came to us with the name Hope, as she was the product of a backyard breeding nightmare and, when rescued, was not expected to live through the night. Her tail had been nibbled terribly by her starving brothers and was saved from amputation only by the heroics of her determined foster Mom.

I learned from her foster Mom that Hope's temperament test indicated that she was going to be a feisty little handful, and oh boy was that ever borne out when we got her home. Never having raised a puppy, I had no idea what to expect. Hope was willful, very vocal and a terror with her brother Darwin who we had adopted from Long Island Golden Retriever Rescue and who, for the first few months, wanted nothing to do with his baby sister. When Hope finally learned what the word NO meant, everything started falling into place. It was obvious to me that she desperately wanted to please, yet had a mind of her own.

I talked about Hope non-stop and began bringing her baby pictures to work. I sensed something extraordinary about her from the moment I got her home; people who I told this to looked at me askance and said, oh really, in what way is she extraordinary? My answer was that she was so completely multidimensional that it was almost impossible to explain. Analytical problem solver, bossy, brassy and bratty, and yet demure and feminine all wrapped into one fuzzy little package.

My husband Eric and I had been toying with the idea of getting out of Manhattan and moving someplace quiet where the dogs would have the life they deserved. I can remember saying to him, "I think Hope is going to be the impetus for us to leave New York City" and him agreeing. An 800 square foot apartment just was not enough for these beautiful animals, and the black top "dog run" in Battery Park City across the street was our only option for socializing them and getting them exercise.

Hope was 14-months-old on September 11, 2001. Our 17th floor apartment was one block from The World Trade Center and faced north into the towers. We left all the windows open on that glorious fall-like day, and both went off to work.

What happened in the next twenty-four hours is a book in itself and, when I look back on it, I still can't believe it happened. We tried in vain to get to the dogs the night of the 11th, but to no avail. National Guardsmen turned us away three blocks from our home. The images and sights of that night will be indelibly etched in my mind forever. The thought that Hope and Darwin were in grave peril was the most gut wrenching, sickening feeling I have ever known and, when coupled with the human loss at the towers, was incomprehensible.

We were finally allowed to enter our apartment in "ground zero" early the morning of the 12th. Hope and Darwin had been alone in the smoke and dust for 24 hours, and our reunion was the stuff dreams are made of. They were just as we had left them, full of spunk and joy, and we could detect no ill effects from their perilous 24 hours in "hell."

It seems Baby Hope and Darwin were going to be country dogs after all. A dream born out of disaster and tragedy on a scale too large to comprehend was realized after we all moved to Northern Virginia and took up residence in an old farmhouse. My husband Eric and I promised Hope and Darwin that we would never go off to work and leave them again and we haven't. I consider every day with my dogs a gift. These beautiful, loving creatures have blessed our lives and gently nudged us in directions we never thought possible.

—*Nan Schramm*

Joe Rodwell and Badger

BADGER

Golden Retriever Rescue of Wisconsin

Joe and I adopted Badger from the golden retriever rescue group last summer and he is the light of our lives. Surrendered to the rescue group by his owners when he was only 10-months-old, Badger was just a great big puppy, full of energy and so playful!

We fell in love with Badger from the very first moment we laid eyes on him, and I think he did too. He fit right into our household as if he'd always been here, even charming our 4 cats who accepted him without so much as a fuss.

Badger is a maniac when it comes to retrieving! He loves his tennis ball and will fetch it as many times as you will throw it! He goes everywhere with us and loves to ride in the front seat of our truck with Joe when he goes on errands. He's a good friend and seems to know when I need a little boost. If I'm upset or have a bad day at work, he makes me laugh and forget what's bothering me. Badger loves to sleep in bed with us, I wish they made a bed bigger than a king size for he is a real bed hog. Badger truly is an amazing dog and we are incredibly lucky to have found him!

—*Lorrie Rodwell*

Dan Riordan and Jeff Steinmann & Sam

SAM

Love A Golden Retriever Rescue

My dog Sam was bred as part of a Future Farmers of America project. After the project was over, he was placed with a farmer who wanted him to ride in the back of his truck, but Sam wanted nothing to do with that. Finally, the farmer had enough, took Sam to the vet and left him there with an advertisement for "free to good home." That's when the rescue group saved him. They cured his heartworms and treated his eye and ear injuries.

I always wanted a dog and, after many months of research, found Sam on the Love a Golden website. After completing the application process and being approved for adoption, I brought Sam home to live with me. He was really worried about all the new noises at first and he missed his foster mom, too. But it didn't take him long before he got used to his new home and began to make friends with the neighbors. Every time he's out in the yard and sees a neighbor, Sam puts his front paws on the fence and stays there until they finally come over to pet him. Then he is the happiest dog in the world.

Sam just graduated from basic obedience class! He was the best dog in the class. He now knows sit, down, stay and he heels like a champion. He also knows up and off; if you extend you arm, he'll jump on it so you don't have to lean over to pet him! Sam made many new friends in basic obedience. Not really with the other dogs, but with the other owners! Sam is definitely a "people dog." He won't play with other dogs if there are people around. I always imagine him thinking, "Why should I bother with that common dog?"

Sam's favorite food is bread of any kind. He loves to eat the heels of the loaf of bread or any bread scrap. I often toss food to him, and he catches it in the air. No vegetables, though. I tossed him a carrot once and he spit it out! Most dogs like attention, but Sam demands it. When someone comes in the door, he goes over to them and leans on their legs. He would stay there forever.

Sam has been a great addition to our home. He is my first dog, so he had to show me the ropes! I'm convinced Sam has spoiled me. I'm afraid no other dog I ever get will be as good as him! Adopting Sam was a great decision. I am very lucky to have a dog like Sam. There is not a day that goes by that I wonder why anyone would have ever given him up.

—Jeff Steinmann

Darcy Dickinson and Sproul

SPROUL

Goldhaven Golden Retriever Rescue

Her owners surrendered the one-year-old golden retriever to the rescue group when they moved to an apartment. But her high-energy personality made it difficult for her to find a new family, and she stayed with the rescue group for six months until we found her on the Internet.

Sergeant Flores and I work in Berkeley for the University of California Police Department. Our Department was looking for a dog to train for our Explosive Ordinance Detection K-9 team. We drove 20 hours in one day to meet and adopt the young Golden, and we named her Sproul after the building that our Police Department is in. Sproul is the perfect dog for our Department, with all the qualities a bomb K-9 must possess. She's very friendly, highly energetic, extremely intelligent, plus she is so darn cute. If I were to compare a regular dog's energy level to Sproul's, it would be like comparing the candle on a birthday cake to fireworks on the Fourth of July.

Sproul and I went through an extensive training program with Sergeant Flores. We trained for what seemed like 24 hours a day, and, in just 8 weeks, we were fully certified through the Police Officer Standards of Training for explosive detection work. Sproul became an official Police K-9 and wears a brass badge on her collar. Her badge number is 99.

Sproul and I have trained in some exciting places. We've trained underneath bridges, on barges, on Alcatraz Island, on airplanes, in airports, on BART (Bay Area Rapid Transit) trains, and in Stadiums. When training near water, Sproul can't resist the urge to jump in and take a quick swim. Her explosive detection ability allows her to meet interesting people and go to exciting places.

Sproul is able to keep people safe by providing bomb sweeps for events and dignitary protection. She is also used in safety talks for children. Balloons titled "Sproul, Everyday Hero" were made with her picture on them to hand out to children at events. Sproul has provided dignitary protection for former President Clinton and other high-ranking officials. She was an instant celebrity at the University and in the community, and her fan club grows larger everyday. Even people who are usually grumpy seem to become full of life when Sproul is around. She brings out the good side in everyone.

Sproul is an official member of the Police Department. I am lucky because I'm the handler. Sproul goes from home to work with me every day. She rides in the extended cab portion of my truck and always has her head on my shoulder when I drive; by the time I get to work my right shoulder is covered in dog hair. When Sproul is not at work, she lives as a family pet. She loves to go for walks, chew on bones and play in the backyard with my other rescue dog Rocky. Sproul is especially good at catching Frisbees. As surprising as it may be, her favorite treat is a banana. She likes all types of fruit, but bananas are her favorite. One time she took a bunch of bananas from the kitchen table, dragged them to a corner and tried to eat them, peel and all; she wasn't very successful.

Sproul is the most amazing dog that I have ever met. She may feel like she was lucky to be rescued, but we are the lucky ones. If you are ever in Berkeley, stop by the UC Berkeley Police Department and meet Sproul.

—Darcy Dickinson

John Bishop and Abbey

ABBEY

Retrieve a Golden of Minnesota

2002 has been "the year from hell" in my life. I had some large business setbacks...my mother passed away...I was diagnosed with cancer...and my business partner lost his foot. Anything that could go wrong has. Abbey has been the only bright spot in my life this year. She is gentle, doesn't bark, is obedient and is my constant companion. I guess if I had grandchildren I would brag on them being perfect but as I don't, I brag on her.

Abbey was a stray in bad shape when the rescue group found her, but she's in great shape now. Everybody says her name should be Shadow, not Abbey, because she follows me everywhere, even to the bathroom! As you can see in the picture, she loves the wave runner. I guess her only downfall is that she is a "not retriever!" I absolutely can't get her to retrieve, no matter what I throw or how hard I try, but she certainly could have worse shortcomings.

I'm thankful to Abbey for being the single bright spot for me in 2002. She is just great.

—John Bishop

Renée and Leon Sankar & Zach

ZACK

Leader Dogs for the Blind

Leon and I were passengers as my daughter drove us to the Leader Dogs for the Blind facility in Rochester, Michigan. It is quite a distance from our home, which gave me time to contemplate my unwillingness to fall in love again with a four-legged friend. I was still hurting from having to put our beloved German Shepherd, Shiloh, to sleep. He was a stray we took in years before and he turned out to be a treasure.

Upon our arrival, an attendant greeted us. We were advised that we would soon be meeting Zack, a Golden Retriever who had flunked out of blind school and needed a home. Although Leon's macular degeneration had not yet resulted in a total loss of vision, the condition had taken a toll on his sight. He, too, was uncertain that he could make a commitment to caring for a new dog.

We were escorted to a large room and asked to sit in the chairs on the far side of the room. Moments later, Zack and the attendant appeared in the doorway. Before we could even stand to greet him, Zack bounded 40 feet, skidding to a stop in front of Leon's legs. It was love at first sight.

Ten years have passed since that "first date." The instinct Zack displayed on that day has never wavered. Our friends are amused when we talk about his large vocabulary and his nature; how the phrase "special delivery" causes Zack to find the paper and deliver it; or that he started barking at approaching humans only after someone broke into the house; the way he makes the rounds with company as if playing the host. We are in love three ways.

—*Renée Sankar*

Appendix A

RESCUER'S CREED

I promise I will take your unwanted animals.
I will heal their wounds, their diseases, their broken bones.
I will give them the medical attention they need and deserve.
I will nurture their starvation and give them a warm place to sleep.

I will spay and neuter them,
vaccinate them against the diseases that can harm them.
I will treat them and honor them.
I will buy them toys, blankets, and balls and teach them to play.
I will speak softly to them.

I will try to teach them not to cry, not to fear, and not to hate.
I will whisper sweet, kind, gentle words into their ears,
while gently trying to stroke their fear, their pain, and their scars away.
I will face their emotional scars and give them time to overcome them.

I will socialize them, potty train them, teach them to be obedient,
show them dignity, and hold their paws,
and stroke their ears if they have endured too much
and walk them over The Bridge,
but most of all I will teach them Love.

—Author Unknown

Golden Rescue on Guard at the Land of Pure Gold
http://landofpuregold.com/rescue.htm

APPENDIX B

ADDENDUM TO THE RESCUER'S CREED

I will do my very best not to hate the animal's breeders or previous owners and to understand that people sometimes act in ways I cannot comprehend for reasons that are deeply personal and seldom fully revealed.

I will empathize with family situations that force a parting with a beloved but four footed family member. I will be true to the trust they place in me to care for their pets properly when they cannot.

I will try to see that in many cases the people need as much compassion as the helpless animals that have been in their care. And if I am unable to do that at the very least I will not take my frustrations and angers out on people who's lives I only touch when they are parting with their animal.

For the humans I come in contact with need my pledge as much as the animals that come into my care.

—*Nancy Holmes*

Appendix C

THE RAINBOW BRIDGE

Just this side of heaven is a place called Rainbow Bridge. When an animal dies that has been especially close to someone here, that pet goes to Rainbow Bridge.

There are meadows and hills for all of our special friends so they can run and play together. There is plenty of food, water and sunshine, and our friends are warm and comfortable.

All the animals who have been ill and old are restored to health and vigor; those who were hurt or maimed are made whole and strong again, just as we remember them in our dreams of days and times gone by. The animals are happy and content, except for one small thing; they each miss someone very special to them, who had to be left behind.

They all run and play together, but the day comes when one suddenly stops and looks into the distance. His bright eyes are intent; his eager body begins to quiver. Suddenly he begins to run from the group, flying over the green grass, his legs carrying him faster and faster.

You have been spotted, and when you and your special friend finally meet, you cling together in joyous reunion, never to be parted again. The happy kisses rain upon your face; your hands again caress the beloved head, and you look once more into the trusting eyes of your pet, so long gone from your life but never absent from your heart. Then you cross Rainbow Bridge together.

—Author Unknown

Appendix D

WEBSITES FOR GOLDEN RETRIEVER RESCUE ORGANIZATIONS

ALASKA

Golden Retriever Rescue of Fairbanks
Fairbanks, AK
www.canineworld.com/grrf/

ARIZONA

Arizona Golden Retriever Connection
Phoenix, AZ
www.azgoldenretrieverconnection.org

Rescue a Golden of Arizona (RAGofAZ)
Phoenix, AZ
www.golden-retriever.org

CALIFORNIA

All Retriever Friends (ARF)
Sunland, CA
www.arfdogs.com

Gold Haven Golden Retriever Rescue
Littlerock, CA
www.golden-rescue.com

Golden Retriever Club of San Diego County Rescue Service
Jamul, CA
grcsd@aol.com

Golden Retrievers in Cyberspace (GriC)
Sunnyvale, CA
www.golden-retriever.com

Golden Retriever Rescue
Leona Valley, CA
www.goldenretrieverrescue.org

Homeward Bound Golden Retriever Rescue and Sanctuary, Inc.
Sacramento, CA
www.homewardboundgoldens.org

NORCAL Golden Retriever Rescue, Inc.
Menlo Park, CA
www.golden-rescue.org

COLORADO

Golden Retriever Freedom Rescue, Inc.
Denver, CO
www.goldenretrieverfreedom.com

Golden Retriever Rescue of the Rockies
Morrison, CO
www.goldenrescue.com

CONNECTICUT

Hudson Valley Golden Retriever Rescue, Inc.
Old Saybrook, CT
Ankrist@aol.com

FLORIDA

Golden Retriever Rescue of Mid-Florida, Inc.
Goldenrod, FL
www.grrmf.org

Tropical Dawg Golden Rescue of Boca Raton, Florida
Boca Raton, FL
www.goldenrecueofsouthflorida.hypermart.net

GEORGIA

Dixie Golden Retriever Rescue
Norcross, GA
www.dixiegoldenretriever.org

Golden Retriever Rescue of Atlanta
Peachtree City, GA
www.grra.com

ILLINOIS

Golden Opportunities Golden Retriever Rescue of Illinois
Carol Stream, IL
www.goldenrescue.org

INDIANA

Golden Retriever Rescue and Community Education (GRRACE)
Brownsburg, IN
www.goldenpaws.org/grrace/grrace.html

Southern Indiana Golden Retriever Rescue
Evansville, IN
www.evv.com/rescue.html

KANSAS

Homeward Bound Golden Retriever Rescue
Olathe, KS
www.kcgoldens.org/rescue.htm

KENTUCKY

Golden Retriever Rescue and Adoption of Needy Dogs (GRRAND)
Louisville, KY
www.grrand.org

LOUISIANA

Old Gold Senior Dog Rescue
Metairie, LA
www.oldgoldrescue.org

MAINE

Golden Retriever Rescue of Maine, Inc.
Jefferson, ME
www.grrom.org

Pine Tree Golden Retriever Rescue
Biddeford, ME
goldenhomes@cybertours.com

MARYLAND

GoldHeart Golden Retriever Rescue, Inc.
Phoenix, MD
www.goldheart.org

MASSACHUSETTS

North East All Retriever Rescue (NEARR)
Watertown, MA
www.nearr.com

Yankee Golden Retriever Rescue, Inc. (YGRR)
Hudson, MA
www.ygrr.org

MICHIGAN

Golden Retriever Rescue of Michigan (GRRoM)
Franklin, MI
www.grrom.com

MINNESOTA

Retrieve A Golden Of Minnesota (RAGOM)
St. Louis Park, MN
www.ragom.org

MISSOURI

Gateway Golden Retriever Rescue, Inc.
St. Louis, MO
www.goldenrescuestlouis.org

Golden Recovery Retrieving Retrievers Rescue
Midwest (GRRRR-Midwest)
Blue Springs, MO
www.goldenrecovery.org

KC Golden Retriever Rescue Rangers
Raymore, MO
www.kcgrrr.petfinder.com

Love A Golden Rescue
St. Louis, MO
www.loveagolden.com

NEBRASKA

Golden Retriever Rescue in Nebraska, Inc. (GRRIN)
Lincoln, NE
www.grrin.org

NEVADA

Companion Golden Retriever Rescue Program—Nevada Chapter
Las Vegas, NV
www.nevadagoldenrescue.org

Las Vegas Golden Retriever Rescue
Las Vegas, NV
keith@h2ovelocity.com

NEW JERSEY

Golden Re-Triever Rescue, Inc. (GRRI-NJ)
Newfoundland, NJ
www.dogsaver.org/grri

NEW MEXICO

Rio Grande Valley Golden Retriever Club
Corrales, NM
pwd@technet.nm.net or Sermasgld@aol.com

NEW YORK

Autumn Valley Golden Retriever Club Rescue
Vestal, NY
wrd@ezaccess.net or Bcrittergetter@aol.com

Golden Retriever Rescue of Central New York, Inc. (GRRCNY)
Jamesville, New York
www.grrcny.org

Golden Retriever Rescue Operated with Love Statewide, Inc.
(GRROWLS)
Syracuse, NY
www.grrowls.org

Long Island Golden Retriever Rescue (LIGRR)
Commack, NY
www.ligrr.org

Peppertree Rescue, Inc.
Albany, NY
www.peppertree.org

NORTH CAROLINA

Gold Creek Golden Retriever Rescue
Liberty, NC
www.gcgrr.com

Golden Retriever Rescue Club of Charlotte (GRRCC)
Charlotte, NC
www.grrcc.com

Triad Golden Retriever Rescue, Inc.
Pleasant Garden, NC
www.tgrr.org

OHIO

Golden Endings Golden Retriever Rescue
Ostrander, OH
www.goldenendings.org

Golden Retriever Club of Greater Toledo Rescue Service
Bowling Green, Ohio
Claws10133@aol.com

Golden Retriever Rescue of Northwest Ohio
Toledo, Ohio
slc4goldens@aol.com

Golden Retrievers In Need Rescue Service, Inc. (GRIN)
Cleveland, OH
www.grinrescue.com

Miami Valley Golden Retriever Rescue
Westville, OH
campbellgold@yahoo.com

OKLAHOMA

Sooner Golden Retriever Rescue
Oklahoma City, OK
www.sgrr.org

OREGON

Golden Bond Golden Retriever Rescue of Oregon
Beaverton, OR
www.goldenbondrescue.com

PENNSYLVANIA

Delaware Valley Golden Retriever Rescue, Inc. (DVGRR)
Sinking Springs, PA
www.dvgrr.org

Golden Retriever Adoptions, Placement and Education (GRAPE)
Ridley Park, PA
www.graperescue.homestead.com

Golden Retriever Rescue of Central Pennsylvania, Inc. (GRRCP)
Centre Hall, PA
www.big-rock.com/grrcp

With A Golden Spirit (WAGS)
Irwin, PA
www.wagsrescue.homestead.com

SOUTH CAROLINA

Foothills Golden Retriever Rescue
Greenville, SC
www.fhgrr.com

Low Country Golden Retriever Rescue (LCGRR)
Mt. Pleasant, SC
www.lcgrr.homestead.com

Midlands Golden Rescue
Columbia, SC
www.concentric.net/~deangbb/midlands.html

TENNESSEE

Heartland Golden Retriever Rescue
Oak Ridge, TN
www.heartlandgoldenrescue.org

Memphis Area Golden Retriever Rescue
Germantown, TN
www.magrr.org

Middle Tennessee Golden Retriever Rescue, Inc.
Mt. Juliet, TN
www.rescueagolden.org

Tennessee Valley Golden Retriever Rescue (TVGRR)
Knoxville, TN
www.tvgrr.com

TEXAS

Brazos Valley Golden Retriever Rescue
Bryan, TX
www.brazosvalleygoldens.com

Dallas/Ft. Worth Metro Golden Retriever Rescue, Inc. (DFWGRR)
Dallas, TX
www.dfwmgrc.org/rescue

Gold Ribbon Rescue
Austin, TX
www.grr-tx.com

Golden Beginnings of Texas, Inc. (GBGRR)
Houston, TX
www.wcnet.net/golden-beginnings-of-texas

Golden Retriever Rescue of North Texas
Dallas, TX
www.goldenretrievers.org

UTAH

Companion Golden Retriever Rescue, North
Jordan, UT
www.slcgoldenrescue.org

Companion Golden Retriever Rescue, North
Paradise, Utah
www.utgoldenrescue.org

VERMONT

RagTag Golden Retriever Rescue
Waterbury Center, VT
www.gatewaytovermont.com/Rescue

VIRGINIA

GRREAT, Inc.
Falls Church, VA
www.grreat.org

Southeastern Virginia GRREAT, Inc. (SEVA GRREAT)
Yorktown Church, VA
www.sevagrreat.org

WASHINGTON

Evergreen Golden Retriever Rescue (EGRR)
Woodinville, WA
www.egrc.org

Inland Empire Golden Retriever Rescue (IEGRR)
Spokane, WA
www.geocities.com/iegrr

WISCONSIN

Golden Retriever Rescue of Wisconsin (GRROW)
Appleton, WI
www.grrow.org

0-595-24989-2

Printed in the United States
1182400003B/170